T5-BYH-149

Die Wende

Peaceful Revolution and
Reunification in Greifswald

Reinhard Glöckner

translated from the German

by David Ward

ISBN-10:   1532801629
ISBN-13:   978-1532801624

AUTHOR'S FOREWORD

This account I drew from my recollection of recent events; it grew out of a wealth of fresh impressions and experiences. Some of it will be regarded later in a different light. I am aware of the extent to which this account corresponds to my point of view at the moment.

Nevertheless, I am convinced that it can make some small contribution to understanding and reflection on the present situation. For that reason, it is presented here to the public.

Greifswald, November 1993

ABOUT THE COVER:
The griffin atop a split oak tree is the emblem of the University and Hanseatic City of Greifswald. The background of blue and white represents the historical colors of Pomerania.

CONTENTS

TRANSLATOR'S NOTE

Translation is usually a collaborative effort, and this book is no exception. I would like to thank Dr. Glöckner for his permission to undertake this project, his support along the way, and his patience with the project's stops and starts. My thanks go as well to Gina Logan, Clarke Haywood, and Esther Ward, who read the translation and offered useful feedback. Their efforts led to improvements in the translation on virtually every page. Thanks are also due to Norwich University for its assistance with publication expenses.

No Violence

Die Wende[1] in Greifswald began for me on the evening of February 17, 1981, in the middle of our living room. As happened every month, one of the discussion circles had gathered at eight o'clock in the parsonage of the congregation of St. Mary at 67 *Friedrich Loeffler Strasse*. I no longer recall what topic was to be discussed that evening. But I do remember exactly how someone brought up Dresden and the commemoration of the night of bombing on February 13, 1943, and the peace service in the *Kreuzkirche* and the candlelight vigil beside the ruins of the *Frauenkirche*. "Why Dresden – why not us as well? The church should do it; both the pastor and the congregation. In Dresden, the bishop was present."

By the end of the evening it had been decided: as part of the congregation, we would hold a peace service of our own, commemorating the peaceful surrender of the city of Greifswald to the Red Army on April 29-30, 1945.

And so it began. At the end of April 1981, this circle hosted the first peace service in the *Jakobikirche* under the motto: civic courage instead of corpse-like obedience.

The peace services took place each April and, during the decade

---

[1] *Die Wende* is one of a handful of German words that will be explained in notes and then remain untranslated throughout Dr. Glöckner's narrative, often because a wealth of specific connotations would be lost with any single English rendering of the word. *Sich wenden* means to turn around or over; *die Wende*, or the turning, is the term former East Germans use for the entire process by which East Germany collapsed, and what remained was integrated into the existing economic, political, and legal structure of the Federal Republic of Germany. It dates from the months leading up to the fall of the Berlin Wall (November 9, 1989), and extending at least until the first elections for the united Germany, in December, 1990. For the purposes of this book, Dr. Glöckner extends these temporal parameters somewhat in both directions.

of peace, which the League of Evangelical Churches in the GDR[2] proclaimed that same year, each November a second peace service gave new meaning to the traditional day of penance as an admonition against war and guilt.

None of us knew that there would be a *Wende*. Long as Stalin's shadow, socialism surrounded us, treacherous and omnipresent the State Security Service (*Stasi*) – and increasingly the military as well – with its stranglehold on businesses and schools. The *Wende* was that we wanted no more to remain silent in our domestic hiding places, but to step forward publicly with our commitment to stand by our belief in civic courage.

Everyone in the circle that evening was for it, including the one who – as I now know – was reporting to the *Stasi*. It was the actual participating that some didn't dare do: "I can't do that to my family; there's no way in my profession; the children – you understand . . . " But some certainly did dare to take action, and we resolved from the outset: dancing on eggshells won't do, we need to speak clearly. And that's what we did.

The bishop was dumbstruck – he never came to a peace service, not once in all those years. Yet every year someone from the diocese came, partly to show solidarity, but also partly to warn us: "This time you've gone too far." Some people in the city held their breath, and often we were given warnings.

But for us, that was the *Wende*: in the middle of the global arms race, we walked with our heads unbowed. A conviction is worth nothing if one isn't prepared to stand up for it. However much it might cost, we were prepared to pay.

A great challenge came in the year 1983 with the resolutions on cruise missiles and atomic warheads. Germany on both sides was the blasting chamber and battlefield of a future holocaust. Drills rehearsing for a nuclear emergency and for the event of war were

---

[2] The East German state abbreviated its name, *Deutsche Demokratische Republik*: DDR. The common English equivalent, GDR, will be used throughout this text.

being held even in the kindergartens. Militarism occupied every soul. State leaders had to make sacrifices just like the teachers did. Before long, the victims would be schoolchildren with their hand-sewn patches that read "Swords to Plowshares."

In Greifswald, too, the *SED*[3] leadership at the county level worked through the principals to intimidate and discipline their pupils. The East German state was betting on the military card; civil defense had top priority. One final show of force was the parade in Berlin on October 7, 1989 – which even included FDJ[4] members from Greifswald carrying concealed weapons. On this fortieth anniversary of the German Democratic Republic, Gorbachev said to Honecker: "He who comes too late will be punished by life." Gorbachev relaxed tensions. He could also have turned out to be a second Brezhnev with the motto "socialism or death."

In these years, intense discussion revolved in other circles as well around the questions that churches in all the world were grappling with: peace, justice, preserving creation; i.e. disarmament and detente, social efforts in the so-called third world, the findings of environmental research. Texts acquired in secret, those of the Club of Rome, for example, served as a basis for the ongoing discussion of these questions. With an eye to Poland and Romania, cognizant of the events in Beijing's Tiananmen Square, we were preparing – without knowing it ourselves – for the *Wende.*

Was it a coincidence that the spring of 1989 found us intensively thinking about the structure, the name, the history of the *Vorpommern*[5] region?

---

[3] *SED (Sozialistische Einheitspartei Deutschlands)* the Socialist Unity Party, the ruling party in the GDR, was the result of an involuntary merger in 1946 of the Social Democrats with the Communist Party within the territory of the GDR.
[4] *FDJ (Freie Deutsche Jugend* or Free German Youth) was the youth organization of the SED-state.
[5] In 1945, Germans were driven out of lands along the Baltic Sea that had been German for centuries: East Prussia and most of *Pommern* (Pommerania). Most of those lands became part of postwar Poland; the

Of course we were not the only ones, but in the fall of 1989 we were largely prepared for the challenges the *Wende* would bring, and almost all our members were on board. As in previous years, there was a large, festive gathering of all the discussion circles on the eve of the new year, 1989. A church sociologist, Erhardt Neubert, had been invited from Jena. He said then, in December, 1988, that in the coming year the GDR would cease to exist. He responded to our questions and doubts with data on the rapidly collapsing economy. We didn't believe him. Nevertheless we had been publicly driving the central message of the *Wende* into the ears of Greifswald's citizens for years: No Violence.

The Church

As the years passed, the Protestant churches in the GDR had no longer been able to withstand the pressure from the state. They had had to bend in response to developments that subjected the respective churches of West Germany and the GDR to very different sets of societal conditions and challenges. And so the League of Evangelical Churches came about as the East German partner to the Evangelical Church in West Germany. In the course of many discussions, debates, and disputes, the League of Evangelical Churches had settled on defining itself as the "Church in Socialism."

In doing so, the church committed itself to the people bound into this blanket system of socialism. There were efforts on behalf of a "church *for* socialism." But in many congregations, these efforts led to an even more vehement rejection of the socialist system.

The provincial church in the Greifswald area (*Landeskirche im Bereich Greifswald*) did one thing: to my knowledge it was the only institution that consistently preserved the identity of the lands and

---

small portion of the region that remained in German hands is referred to by locals as *Vorpommern*, which means something like pre-Pommerania, or the part that leads to *Pommern* proper.

people of Pomerania that had remained German.

Although it was forced to call itself the Evangelical Provincial Church Greifswald (*Evangelische Landeskirche Greifswald*), it always did what it was able, in order to keep the *Vorpommern* region intact, and as soon as it seemed conceivable, it returned to the name Pomeranian Evangelical Church.

It stood up for a people who had had to endure the postwar years under particularly difficult circumstances and had had to repay war costs dearly again and again.

But the relationship of our regional church to socialism, to ideology, party and state apparatus was ambivalent. Top church leaders above all had been particularly impressed with the advantages of accommodation for the institutional interests of the church. The permissions and funds that might have been acquired by the Evangelical churches in the neighboring districts of Rostock and New Brandenburg were sometimes awarded within the Greifswald area, to the detriment of the *Mecklenburg* provincial church. We know today that the good behavior of a small group at the head of the provincial church extended to the brink of collaboration with the State Security Service, yet it was easy to guess as much at the time, and even to read it indirectly in occurrences and events. In the individual congregations, in the ranks of the synods, among those employed in the consistory, and even among the members of the church leadership, a controversy arose over the path taken by the bishop and his team, which led to severe disruptions and even to a breakdown of trust.

Like very many other Christians, we also carefully watched the factional squabbles, the acts of censorship, the prohibitions and confiscations that made every issue of the church newspapers in those last years into a suspenseful adventure and a political barometer. As pastor to the congregation of St. Mary in Greifswald and the person responsible for the extensive evening and weekend work involved in renovating our *Marienkirche*, I was made to feel precisely the difference between our project and the building and finances at the Greifswald Cathedral. They had very generous funding, by GDR standards, under the aegis of the bishop on the one hand, and of the Rostock District *SED* party leadership on the other.

As a member of the synod and of the church's governing board, I had the clear sense that the mutual cooperation of state party and bishop was furthering the construction project, but at the same time in the congregations it strained peoples' trust beyond the limit. Even within the governing board, quarrels broke out when – with only a few days' notice, and just weeks before we celebrated the re-dedication of the *St. Nikolai* Cathedral in Greifswald – the bishop announced that the First Secretary of the Socialist Unity Party of Germany and Chairman of the State Council, Comrade Erich Honecker, would be taking part in the church service in the cathedral. Even in the working out of each detail, the discussions within the church leadership were right at the breaking point. Only after the great event, which had placed the whole city of Greifswald under the banner of the Russian Prince Potemkin, did an uproar ensue.[6]

Erich Honecker wanted to make use of the event on the national stage, so he was having a reply to Bishop Dr. Gienke published in *Neues Deutschland*, the official daily newspaper. For this reason, he asked the bishop if the bishop's earlier letter of thanks regarding the dedication of the cathedral could be published beside his own letter. And so we, as members of the governing board, learned from *Neues Deutschland* not only that – and how – our bishop had expressed his thanks to the head of state and party, but also that in this letter he had complained to the general secretary of the atheist Socialist Unity Party, the same Erich Honecker, about his own church newspaper (newsletter) and its reporting.

This unbelievable fact was the last straw. The bishop met with open mistrust. Some members of the governing board gathered, excluding other members whose associations with the *Stasi* were now

---

[6] Pastor Glöckner is referring to the phony village facades allegedly constructed by a Russian general, Grigory Potemkin, in 1787 to conceal from visiting dignitaries the abject poverty of the peasants.

known. The revolt within the governing board was isolated with the help of the bishop's team. The revolt that followed, in the synod, he was no longer able to contain.

In September, 1989, that mistrust was obvious to all. At the next synod, on November 4, the bishop lost a vote of no confidence, which resulted in his resignation.

Thus in the regional church, the *Wende* had its beginning in June 1989 and, beneath the still present roof of the socialist state, it was a process laden with tremendous tension.

This tension was palpable in the political climate in general, especially after Erich Honecker's deputy, Egon Krenz, welcomed the mass murder of protesters on Tiananmen Square in *Beijing* in June, 1989, as an act of securing the peace – and after economic and military contacts with Ceaucescu's Romania were clearly strengthened in August and September of 1989. A joke began circulating: Berlin's Alexanderplatz was to be re-named "Square of Heavenly Peace" – Tiananmen. In this life-threatening climate of socialist peace, the Pomeranian Evangelical Church left the path of accommodation and servility.

The First *Wende* – *Das neue Forum*

Peace services took place in many cities at regular intervals. The worship services in Leipzig each Monday were well attended. Party and state confronted those who attended, cordoned off, blocked access, exercised force. Nevertheless, the services had to be expanded to include other churches in Leipzig in order to accommodate the crowds of people. Finally, it reached the point where there were massive demonstrations following the Leipzig worship services, so that by October 9 the question hung in the air: will they fire on the crowd or not?

A few clear-headed men on both sides prevented the massacre that supposedly had already been ordered. Unlike in Romania, and unlike what we had come to expect from Erich Honecker, there was no bloodshed. Instead there was a revolution on evenings and weekends. In a regular series of peace services and demonstrations, massive pressure was exerted on the socialist authorities. At an astonishing pace, the rotten and rigid skeleton of state and party fell apart piece by piece, like a house of cards. It fell apart from the Elbe to Vladivostok.

In the north of the GDR, little happened at first. Already gas stations in the south had begun refusing gas to cars with northern license plates: "When are you going to start? What's wrong with you?"

The evangelical pastors of Greifswald decided to hold peace services every Wednesday. The first such service took place on October 18. People crowded into the cathedral, until there was scarcely room to stand. Of course the *Stasi* was well represented, too. In the weeks that followed, the *Jakobikirche* was also filled for a parallel service at the same hour. At the end of the service on October 18, Dr. Poldrack read aloud a first statement from *Neues Forum*. Then, when he left the church, I asked several young men I knew to follow him, so that he would have assistance should anything happen to him. When, after the service, I stepped out onto the street myself, Herr and Frau Kuessner were standing there on Domstrasse. At the moment I walked up to them, they lit their candles. Then we set out, and thousands followed in hour-long marches through the city: past the *SED* county headquarters, past the police headquarters on Brinkstrasse – police teams were standing at the ready, and the *Stasi* chief in Greifswald, Comrade Erfurt, came out to meet the march. "Democracy–now or never" – "Turn off the TV, come out in the street" – "Come join us" – the crowd chanted and marched out as far as *Tolstoistrasse* and back again to the cathedral. Those returning from work by train spontaneously began a new march, gathering in the southern part of the city, then following *Pieckallee* and *Petershagenallee* to the center of town. At *Platz der Freiheit*, Freedom Square, the police were assembled. But they withdrew, and so this march came to an end in front of city hall. There, late in the evening, the mayor's staff stood in front of the door and had a discussion with the crowd. "We need a forum for many conversations," people were saying. The churches were suggested. Then the city council offered to mediate and arranged for the large dining hall at the university to be made available for the coming debates and discussions. Starting that evening, and for several weeks that followed, a regular sequence of events emerged: peace service, demonstration, forum.

It was no wonder that GDR-wide the masses of people were calling for a "new forum." The discussions were heated and many voices were heard. People vented their anger at the party and its subordinate organizations, at corrupt functionaries who were willing to use violence against the people. Many topics were energetically discussed. On November 9, discussion centered around expanding travel permits: "The government still hasn't got the point" – "their last proposal isn't worth laughing about, let alone discussing." Such was the mood in the dining hall. Since I had an appointment elsewhere at 8pm, I left. On the street, I learned what was happening in Berlin. Returning to the filled hall, I was able to pass a slip of paper to the speaker: "The wall and the border of the GDR are open." That same night, the first Greifswalders drove to West Berlin.

These weeks were the great period of forums. It was the great period of *Neues Forum*. For in the midst of this almost universal movement for renewal, there were everywhere, and thus also in Greifswald, small groups who were determined to shape this process with the goal of a renewed society, of a better GDR, partly of a more humane socialism, partly of incorporating the ideals of both German states into a constitution they wished for.

It was mainly church members and theologians, people from the theater world, writers, and intellectuals in general who gathered *Stasi* informants and all – in living rooms, then in the packed *Lutherhof* meeting hall, and finally, after issuing an open invitation to the public, in the *Jakobikirche*, which was filled to capacity. The people all expected proposals, suggestions, appeals, an orientation for their powerful desire. They sat up front in the sanctuary, among them a sprinkling of old comrades. Dr. Poldrack sat there, and several activists of the new movement, but also Dr. Jonas, a nimble thinker from city hall who was rooted in the old guard.

Their effort deserved to be honored. *Neues Forum* was to be open to everyone, and it was to really represent the people. Thus the basis of their work should reflect these priorities – in its form as well. Taking overly great care, and weighing each detail with a gold scale in order to balance the new justice and democracy, participants in the podium discussion outdid one another with formal considerations and strove to come up with guidelines for a new charter. Before the eyes of this huge audience, they missed the target, which was to put into words what the people wanted. Instead, they spent hours tinkering with a framework that, in the long run, could be accepted by only a few. Although this group of opposition intellectuals was the hope and the voice of the masses from the start and for a crucial period thereafter, in the population as a whole it represented only a small minority, and so it quickly became just one interest group among others – the "*Neues Forum.*" Its almost daily working groups were completely overburdened and did their best. Two main issues emerged: grass roots democracy and the environment. In the local elections on May 6, 1990, *Neues Forum* received eight percent of the votes in Greifswald, one member became president of *Bürgerschaft*; another was second mayor, and a caucus of five sat in the city council, where soon they were able to make far-reaching resolutions without the prior knowledge, or approval, of their membership at large.

Of lasting significance was an array of groups that emerged from *Neues Forum*, some of which remain active today, though not all are still tied to *Neues Forum*. In January 1993, large segments of *Neues Forum* joined together with the West German Green Party under the name "*Bündnis 90 – Grüne*" (Alliance '90 – Green Party), in order to surpass the five percent threshold and be seated in the *Bundestag*.

Mutually contradicting tendencies are evident between the party's fundamentalists and its pragmatists; for example, in regard to formally recognizing the constitution or responding to financial strains.

The Second *Wende* – Germany, United Fatherland

After a resolute phalanx led by the intellectuals, risking profession and career, life and limb, had broken through the barriers of ideology and *Stasi*, of police, military and, above all, of the civil conflict army titled *Betriebskampfgruppen* (workplace battle groups), people poured into the streets like water through a breached dike. "We are the people" was their battle cry. "We are one people" was the first shift in the direction of the general public's desires. It was no longer dangerous to go into the streets and call for what everyone wanted: national unity, the *Deutschmark*, the banana[7]. Especially after the borders were opened on November 9, conflicting messages were being chanted in the demonstration marches: "Democracy – now or never" the ones shouted along with all the others; "Germany, united fatherland" shouted the others along with the ones. For now, they were all united, but instead of the homemade banners and signs with their carefully thought out slogans, increasingly there were black/red/gold flags – with the emblem of the GDR carefully removed; soon the old German imperial flag appeared, the black/white/red, and even the Prussian black/white. Noteworthy was that nobody shouted ""Deutschland Deutschland über alles"; instead the dominant motto was the phrase from the official text of the GDR national hymn, which had been suppressed for years: "*Deutschland, einig Vaterland* – Germany, united fatherland."

No longer was it a matter of debating the threadbare ideals of

---

[7] Since the East German currency was not convertible, some imported commodities that West Germans took for granted, like tropical fruit, were not available in the East.

socialism. Washed away was the *SED*'s principle of the party's leading role – swallowed up the successor *SED* regime under Egon Krenz. The government under Hans Modrow held just a little longer, and then, after only half a year of a democratic GDR under the cabinet assembled by Lothar de Maizière, came incorporation into the Federal Republic of Germany as prescribed in article 23 of the Basic Law.[8]

The majority of the people had looked right past *Neues Forum* and decided in favor of the affluent West. Elemental desires emerged and found expression in consumer behavior with the DM 100 of "welcome money" that each GDR citizen received on the other side of the border; with the exploitation of the GDR-Mark / D-Mark exchange rate, both officially and on the black market; with the exchange (at 1:1) of the first four thousand marks in savings for shiny used cars. None other than the old comrades began playing a game of misdirection – like a thief himself shouting "Stop, thief!" They painted "Nazis, get out!" on walls; and it wasn't long before, in the first stirrings of national fervor, there came outbreaks of chauvinism and right-wing extremism. In Greifswald, a crowd of children and youths with shaved heads soon appeared on the streets, calling themselves National Socialists of Greifswald.

The ideals of *Neues Forum* paled in the face of these unleashed instincts. The democracy of the people turned out to be the rule of the people and of their conflicting interests. Often enough, these interests were expressed in boundless aggression. In the days of the round table, and in the first months of the democratically elected city council and administration, there were plenty of anonymous telephone calls – not a few among them including death threats and other forms of intimidation. Within a short time, our city saw a hundred bomb threats aimed at all sorts of targets: railroad station, children's hospital, Christmas services, theater performances, city hall,

---

[8] The word translated here as incorporation, "Anschluss", is the same term euphemistically used by the National Socialists to describe the only partially voluntary incorporation of Austria into the German *Reich* in 1938.

and flea market. There were several arson attacks on refugee housing. Fortunately, the fires were put out in time. Eagerly, the foolish hands of youthful and adult cowards scrawled their logos on the walls of houses and other buildings: "Germany die," "Shit has always been brown," "String up Krause," "Put leftists in concentration camps." All sorts of rhyming and unrhymed nonsense in a jumble of words and drawings gives a faithful reflection of the muddied and muddled state of many minds. The gabled building on the north end of the Greifswald market square, restored with such care and now rented by *Deutsche Bank*, is just one of their favorite targets. Just now it is respendent with the shrill colors of balloons full of paint tossed at its upper stories.

One late evening, months ago, I caught one of these vandals. Hung with chains and insignia, a pale, narrow-faced adolescent had hidden himself in the deep shadows of a vacant lot full of weeds. He tried out some anarchist slogans and denied his identity. He was really terrified of his father.

But the fathers and mothers held firm to their professions and workplaces. In the streets they were brave and demanded a new state, a new city. But at work, people were still and did what they were told. There was no great change there. The old bosses by the grace of Honecker kept things firmly in hand. "Without us, you'll soon be broke." They appeared as the real vanguard of the market economy, and whoever had spoken out too loudly in the streets was now left standing outside the factory gate, an unemployed cost-cutting measure, welcomed with a smile, perhaps, by a former *Stasi* agent who has found a new line of work overseeing a new unemployment office.

At work, nothing had changed. People could be blackmailed even more easily when their very jobs were at stake. They had maintained workplace discipline even during the *Wende*, holding demonstrations and marches after hours, and they continued to be industrious and well-behaved, obedient and asking for only modest improvements – and completely befuddled when, sooner or later, personal change reached them in the form of unemployment. What now?

Partnership

Before the *Wende*, the rumor circulated in Greifswald that *Strasse der Freundschaft*, literally Street of Friendship, was going to be renamed *Strasse der SED*, because there one could find harbingers of a market economy that was not social: **S**hopping, **E**xquisite, **D**elicacies. With a targeted assortment of high-quality goods, state-run shops aimed to skim off the surplus money, especially any hard currency from relatives in the West, into the state's coffers. Even the firmest of socialist principles had to yield before the hard *Deutschmark*. Under this pressure, hard-won and painstakingly negotiated concessions became possible. Under this pressure, in 1988 Honecker allowed the city of Greifswald to accept a sister city partnership with a West German city. After some back and forth, the choice fell on Osnabrück, and since then a bizarre ritual developed consisting of infrequent, highly official receptions of delegations between the two cities, straightjacketed within the framework of a charter whose carefully phrased language was aimed more at impeding than at enabling. With great openness the city council and administration of Osnabrück tried to make as many contacts as possible. The *Stasi* and the Party supervised with jealous eyes every encounter with representatives of the "West German class enemy." Nothing was allowed to happen apart from the fixed protocols. One weak point in their control was the churches, and during each visit, the guests from the West asked to be shown around a church, where more open questions met with more open answers.

One member of the Greifswald city council, Herr Dornheck, fell victim to one of these encounters. He had met with an Osnabrück representative for a beer outside the protocols. That cost him a disciplinary hearing, as a result of which he gave up his position on the council. City partnerships in those days were like crocuses peeking out of the snow.

In October and November of 1989, the city council members of Greifswald tried to exploit the now more open contacts in order to strengthen their old powers. But quickly a small group from among the new forces arranged an agreement with the partners in Osnabrück that every step should be coordinated with the new spokespersons in Greifswald. And that is just what happened.

The first assistance was directed at the *Neues Forum* and equipped an organizational office with suitable technology so that the time-consuming detail work of communications could be handled a bit more efficiently. In a back room at the *Nationale Front*, at *Domstrasse* 38, a small office was established. There Herr Salewski and Frau Fermum and a number of others got off to a lively start, spreading word of the most important agreements for the new development in Greifswald.

Soon after the fall of the Wall on November 9, there was a large gathering in the university dining hall: a substantial number of city council members and administrators from Osnabrück appeared, explained their backgrounds and party affiliations, and above all, informed themselves about the events that had shaped the *Wende*. They took part in a meeting in which, naturally, questions and answers played a large role, especially including negotiations concerning the composition of the planned round table. Those were the first steps, taken in the presence of our partners, toward including the city administration, including the old city council, in new mutual agreement procedures, which then shaped the period leading up to the local elections in May, 1990.

Late into the night the discussions continued, mostly in private homes. The city partnership was filling with energy and life like a river after a cloudburst. Many group encounters, between school classes and choruses, between teachers and educators, from family to family, also from church congregation to congregation, have taken place since. Each step of the change has been followed closely and accompanied by assistance in word and deed.

Later, when the new city legislature had been elected, and the new city administration was being formed, an enormously helpful program of organizational assistance was set in motion. First off, Herr Pösse and Herr Bouché from the Osnabrück city administration helped us to put in place a new charter and thus a legal basis for our city administration. Whole departments from the Greifswald city hall spent whole days and weeks in Osnabrück, learning to work with the new administrative structures and mechanisms. Again and again, officials and specialists came from Osnabrück to Greifswald to help set up whole administrative sections to replace our old offices and departments. In November, 1990, the department heads met with the mayor and the city manager in our partner city for a retreat. Herr Bouché relocated to Greifswald – although still receiving his salary for the moment from his former employers – and took charge of the city planning office. In response to our general inquiry about legal assistance, Herr Ahrenskrieger came to Greifswald, where he has assumed direction of the legal office and has since begun to put down roots in our city. An extremely important contribution in the first months was made by the two emissaries the two cities exchanged, Herr Wächter and Herr Rieger. Herr Westerhaus (social services) and Herr Fitschen of the Osnabrück city council (chief administrator and head of the department of internal administration) were delegated to Greifswald for months. Many months were spent by Herr Helbing on questions concerning the administration of real property, Herr Goehrs with the working group for the restitution of properties owned by the city, and Herr Thermath in setting up a corporation – since defunct – to promote economic development in three localities: Wolgast county, and both the county and city of Greifswald. Many of these activities were paid for out of Osnabrück's municipal budget – an expense that ran into the millions.

The most visible sign of this assistance appeared one morning in front of the Greifswald city hall, and it filled the entire market square: nine city buses from Osnabrück entered public service in our city. This aid, which was visible every day, everywhere, became so much a part of daily life in Greifswald that many of our citizens eventually forgot the origin of these buses from our partner city. But it has not been forgotten that in this difficult time of transition no one helped us as much and as intensively as did our partner city, Osnabrück. The very fact that the Ernst Moritz Arndt University in Greifswald succeeded in re-establishing a faculty of Jurisprudence and putting it on a sound footing we owe in important ways to the prompt and thorough assistance the University of Osnabrück provided.

Apart from relationships within families and churches, there proved to be no stronger justification for speaking of "brothers and sisters" than in the partnerships of cities.

Of course, it is not surprising that some of the first investors came from Osnabrück to Greifswald, and a network of interests has formed that is introducing what promise to be lasting associations of their own kind between the two cities.

Yet just as Osnabrück has other partner cities in Angers, Derby, Haarlem, Twer, Evansville, and Pisa, that all have thus taken an interest in Greifswald, Greifswald has a series of partnerships that significantly expand our citizens' horizons and our city's options.

For many years, a lively partnership had been maintained between the universities of Lund and Greifswald. And so it was a special pleasure for the citizenry and the administration when a partnership with the Swedish city of Lund was established and then confirmed in a solemn ceremony on October 7, 1990 – in the afterglow of German unification a few days earlier – with an exchange of signatures in Lund. This partnership has been fruitful, especially in the schools. In addition, relations between *Vorpommern* and southern Sweden have a centuries-long tradition, which cannot be filled enough with new life.

During the cold war, Finland had a special intermediary position between the two hostile camps. So it came that, quite early on, an official partnership was set up with the city of Kotka – hence the street named *Kotka-Ring* in the *Ostsee* section of our city. Since I was a member of the city council even before the *Wende*, I was once invited to a formal dinner with the delegations from Kotka and Greifswald in our *Boddenhus*. Never before and never since have I experienced a ceremony as sterile, frosty, and devoid of substance as this reception. Hans Christian Andersen memorably captured such an atmosphere in his fairy tale of the snow queen. Just that icy and frustrating is how the encounter between Kotka and Greifswald imprinted itself onto my memory. Since, for Western Pomerania, the line Scandanavia – Berlin – Prague – Budapest is of particular importance, and since the ports Sassnitz and Mukran comprise the head of that line, Finland is of particular importance for the economic development of *Vorpommern*, insofar as Mukran is equipped to convert railroad cars from European gauge to the wide gauge that was the old Russian – and therefore present-day Finnish – standard. Would it be possible to construct in Finland a port facility especially for the rail converter in Mukran? This question led me in November 1990 to visit Kotka, which, together with Hamina, is the second largest port in Finland, equidistant from Helsinki and St. Petersburg. Especially the German consul in Kotka, Herr Zimmermann, took a great interest in this question and continues to be involved in these efforts. In the parliament and the city administration, my visit was met with surprise and friendly curiosity, for in these places Consul Zimmermann and others had already developed a good and lively partnership between Kotka and the German port city of Lübeck. This partnership with the Federal Republic of Germany had stood in competition with the GDR partnership with Greifswald. The Greifswald partnership had been carried essentially by the communist faction in the Kotka city parliament and promoted by the very energetic former Greifswald medical student, Dr. Tiusanen. Now, after the *Wende*, several questions had arisen. How much sense did it make to continue the communist-led city partnership with Greifswald, and should they have two partnerships in Germany? That wouldn't make much sense.

Thus the tendency was away from Greifswald and toward Lübeck. But Dr. Tiusanen and his faction – as well as his circle of friends – had no intention of giving up on Greifswald. Neither did Consul Zimmermann, who spoke up against giving up on what had been a very restrictive situation at the very moment that we in Greifswald with our new possibilities were finally able to take up genuine and lively relations. And so my visit, and the friendly attention it aroused, came at just the right time to preserve this partnership for Greifswald. Since then, the sailing ship *Greif* has visited Kotka as our emissary. And from Kotka, as well, visitors have come to us. Relations are still weak and difficult as a result of the geographical and linguistic distance that separates us, but here a good bit of future has been opened up.

Likewise dating back to socialist times were regular encounters between the music schools on the one hand, and the fire departments on the other, with the Polish city of Goleniow. These relations were deliberately cultivated and approved by the *Bürgerschaft* and the senate in Greifswald, and so both the president and the mayor of Goleniow had made frequent visits to Greifswald and thus maintained relations across the problem-laden border along the Oder River and opened possibilities that are still receiving too little attention.

In the files of the Greifswald city hall yet another partnership, a rather undefinable one, turned up: Bethune. No one knew where it was; no one remembered anything about it. And yet at one point negotiations in this direction must have taken place. For by a circuitous route a message reached us, inquiring why a letter from Bethune had not received a reply. However, we were unable to find any such letter, although we did succeed in locating Bethune on a map, in the north of France. At the conference for trans-border interaction held in Cottbus in the summer of 1991, I found myself conversing with Monsieur Martin, an enthusiastic advocate of city partnerships. He brought new life to our contact with Bethune. And soon we were surprised by Bethune's energetic mayor and his delegation, and by a charming and clever initiative on their part, which quickly swept aside our hesitant reserve and has in the meantime helped bring about several fruitful encounters on both sides. Soon a symbolic picture of our befriended city, Bethune, graced the wall beside the chair of Greifswald's chief mayor, indicating what a favorable, strategic location this city has, south of the channel and right at the exit of the tunnel between the European continent and Great Britain. There will never be a tunnel to Greifswald, but the world of the French language and the amicable, open vitality of our partners will do us less-flexible North Germans some good – as well as piquing and promoting our mutual interest.

It is in the interest of our city to officially promote these partnerships and to cultivate and continue the amicable tone and goodwill that Frau Melzig, our first partnerships coordinator, has put in place. Initiatives to propose or request partnerships with cities in the Baltic states have thus far yielded no meaningful results.

Sword and Shield of the Party – the State Security Service

People often have less respect for a farmer than for the dog he keeps chained in the yard. The state security service – its full name, *Staatssicherheitsdienst*, usually shortened in popular usage to *Stasi* – was the dog not of the state but of the *SED*: sword and shield of the party. It didn't bark much, but it certainly did a lot of sniffing and biting – all at the state's expense, but in the service of the party's comrades. And so it is understandable that the party did not usually recruit its snoops and sniffers from within its own ranks. After all, a non-comrade was less conspicuous and more trustworthy. Besides, now that the change has come, it's much easier to forget that every party member carries his share of responsibility as the *Stasi*'s employer. Yes, with all its official and unofficial participants, the *Stasi* is serving now as lightning rod and scapegoat – being truly the shield of the party and its comrades more than ever.

Many were the tasks undertaken by "Listen and Look, Inc.", as popular slang labeled the *Stasi*. In Greifswald, as elsewhere, there was no such thing as an admission to university studies or to a career as research assistant, no permission to visit relatives in the West, and certainly no business trip into countries outside the Warsaw Pact – without a thorough review leading to the required evaluation of the applicant, his activities and his surroundings. The population reacted like rabbits in an open field: they kept their heads down and tried not to attract attention.

As happened elsewhere, in Greifswald the *Stasi* laid claim to the traditional court building at *Domstrasse* 7. "What is right is what is useful to the party" was the silent message of this red brick building. The court was banished to the rear courtyard of *Domstrasse* 20. The main building at that address housed the comrade/professors of Marxism-Leninism. For centuries, there had been a faculty of Law in Greifswald – but not under socialism. State and justice had become instruments of power for the so-called class of workers. This was the official line of instruction, because according to Marxist teachings, socialism is the dictatorship of the proletariat. However, we encountered the so-called class of workers almost exclusively in the guise of a cliquish troupe of aging (and eventually aged) *SED* functionaries who saw themselves as their own avant garde. The most insidious instrument of their dictatorship was the *Stasi*, so greatly feared that one did best not to speak of them at all. That topic was taboo. It's best not to provoke a dog that bites.

And so I was all the more astonished when, in April of 1989, the manager of a store owned by the people began speaking to me, and, although we had almost never spoken with each other before, he told me that the husband of one of his saleswomen had given up his job in order to enlist in the *Stasi*. The manager had said to her, "How can you go out in the spring of 1945 and buy a brown shirt?" and then had been shocked at his own boldness.

Even in the period of the *Wende*, it took a while before the *Stasi* became a topic of open discussion. There had been calls from within the demonstration marches: "Make the *Stasi* do factory work!" But it wasn't until the peace service on November 15th that I brought up the subject, so that it inevitably became the topic of our next forum. This forum was among the most turbulent events in an turbulent period. The great university dining hall was packed solid, and the large ground floor hall, where the discussion was carried over loudspeakers, was nearly as full. Not only the *Stasi* bosses from Greifswald had shown up, the leading *Stasi* comrades from the district of Rostock were also seated on the podium and dominated the discussion. They soon found themselves engaged in a discussion with the gathered crowd, with countless contributions and interjections from the audience. A medical director was supposed to moderate. But he was rejected by the audience as not impartial. So it fell to me to direct the conversation. Quickly the discussion became energetic and nearly impossible to control. Many more questions were passed forward on slips of paper. I still see the theology student before me who shouted up at the *Stasi* chief of the Rostock district, "Lie, you're lying, all lies!" And when asked his name, he gave his name, address, and added much that he remembered of previous conversations and/or interrogations. The euphemistic and vacuous explanations of the *Stasi* comrades made the crowd more and more angry. I noted, though, that the results so far were satisfactory, because the *Stasi* was still fully active and its minions were giving the prescribed answers, so we could be sure that the *Stasi* as an organization was still fully under arms. *Wende* or no *Wende*, nothing was different there yet at all. For the fact that the State Security Service had now become the Agency for National Security was clearly not a substantial change but merely cosmetic.

It didn't take long before one speaker at the microphone called upon the government to take all police authority away from the *Stasi*. I called for a vote on the question: the majority was in favor. And to make the proportion of votes visible, I called for a show of hands. All the arms went up. I looked across the room and it was like looking across a wheat field. There were six no votes and fourteen undecided. That was the turning point for the assembled comrades of the *Stasi*.

They suddenly looked pale and very unsure of themselves. As if something in some apparatus had clicked, suddenly the whole climate had changed. And then came the demand: "We want to go into the *Stasi* cellars."

The meeting had begun at 7:30. At midnight, I was part of a small group chosen by acclaim that entered the rooms in the basement of *Domstrasse* 7, accompanied by both *Stasi* and the press. Of course, there was nothing to find: coal, and to our surprise, a sauna, then cellar space and several detention cells that supposedly hadn't been occupied for years. One of the students did find something: the old, official door sign, "State Security Service, County Office, Greifswald" and with it the *Stasi* emblem. He was allowed to take it. Soon thereafter it was auctioned in West Berlin, the proceeds going to a children's center in Greifswald. What we were intent on finding – that files were being burnt – was not in evidence.

But because the destruction of files was indeed taking place, a brave group undertook an initiative. On December 4, they entered the offices at *Domstrasse* 7 and sealed the file cabinets. The mayor (*SED*) had given them the authority to do so. The county director of the people's police (*SED*) provided protection for them, the state's attorney (*SED*) had issued a search warrant. A short time later, a reading of the files began under the direction of Dr. Thomas Meyer. The comrade *Stasi* officers were on the job and at their desks, of course, and beside them sat the twenty or so people who examined the files and had the *Stasi* comrades explain the abbreviations to them. They explained more than that, telling the readers, for example, "If you so much as touch this file, then your life will no longer be safe."

On the basis of these and other threats, a few of the volunteer readers were deterred from continuing with the examination, which went on for many days. Finally, the examining group barred the *Stasi* from entering the offices. That led to one of the most critical situations in the period of *Wende* in Greifswald. But despite the support of a delegation from Berlin, the *Stasi* officers did not succeed in overcoming the firm resolve of the examining group. Many of those who read the files felt physically befouled and besmirched by the denunciations, defamations and breaches of trust – down to the most intimate areas – that they had read.

In our city of about 65,000 inhabitants, there were files on 22,000 persons, although the dossiers under a number of initial letters had disappeared. Everything possible and impossible was there to read in the reports. For example, everyone who had not participated in the local elections, in May, 1989, had received a special mark in their file. The examiners took the time and counted the marks. They documented at least 1,109 non-voters. At the time, the newspapers had published the number 429. The mayor responsible for the elections, Ewald, was asked, whereupon he gave the judges a full statement, implicating himself as well. He stated before an investigative commission the next day that a few days *before* the election he had received a slip of paper from the head of the district party office with the election results for Greifswald. On the evening of election day, then, he reported the data from this slip back to Rostock as the official election results. The mayor was fined 3,000 marks GDR for election fraud. But we – and for the same reason, the citizens of Erfurt as well – now knew how the voters had been defrauded. And we also knew back then that we could almost surely conclude who committed the election fraud in Dresden: the mayor in his domain and Hans Modrow, the first secretary of the party leadership in that district. But in the meantime, Modrow had become chief executive of the *Wende*, and later would become a member of the *Bundestag* in the unified Germany.

So there were already results that could be published. A little book about the *Stasi* investigations in Greifswald was quickly published under difficult conditions and received a good deal of attention. Later, the *Stasi* files from Greifswald were transferred to Waldeck outside of Rostock. In all the German Democratic Republic, the Hanseatic City of Greifswald was the only community whose inhabitants themselves reviewed the files of the local *Stasi*.

In much the same way that the group led by Dr. Thomas Meyer examined the *Stasi* files, there was a group, led by Dr. Drenckhan, that reviewed the files in the *SED* county headquarters, one group for the files in the city hall, and another group for the papers of the county school board. The *Stasi* files at the nuclear power plant Lubmin were reviewed as well. In this regard, the round table soon had resolved two things: The fifty-two official employees of the *Stasi* in Greifswald were fired, and the building at *Domstrasse* 7 was promised to the university for its music students, whose spaces were not only dilapidated, they were already crumbling.

"Make the *Stasi* do factory work!" they had shouted in the streets. As the first to become unemployed, and having excellent contacts, former *Stasi* people soon appeared as officials or even directors of newly-established unemployment offices, or at the private security companies that were suddenly springing up everywhere. Some have permission to carry weapons even today, because Federal German law recognizes no reason why a person without a police record should not be allowed to possess and make use of a firearm. I am convinced that the *Stasi* people have jobs, no matter how high unemployment rises. And in a variety of areas, there are signs that old *Stasi* connections are being re-established and suddenly coming up with substantial amounts of foreign capital, sometimes in the millions, for local investment.

The *Round Table*

"No Violence" was the slogan, and the *Wende* ran its course peacefully in the GDR. The others didn't shoot at us, nor we at them. And so we will have to get along with them as neighbors, until the end of our lives. That is the peaceful but bitter truth. The first and most valid expression of that truth was manifest in the round table, which was set up under the leadership of both the Evangelical and the Catholic Church for the whole of the GDR. Soon regional round tables were established in many locations. There was one in Greifswald.

The *SED*-mayor, Wellner, conferred with several partners and called together the Greifswald round table for the first time on December 11, 1989. Representatives of the newly formed groups and parties were invited, but so were the existing parties and organizations that already had seats and votes in the city assembly, so that there was practically a parity of the old and the new. As leaders, the Protestant superintendant, Wackwitz, and I were proposed. Mayor Wellner and his two deputies, Dr. Schulz and Dr. Jonas, also sat at the table.

The mayor was still bound by the decisions of the city assembly. The old system remained in place and operated until the election of the new *Bürgerschaft* on May 6, 1990. The city administration remained in office until the first meeting of the *Bürgerschaft* on May 29, and in these last weeks it had free rein without democratic oversight. The counsel and the resolutions of the round table were without legal force, and yet the mayor declared himself bound by them; also the city assembly followed the recommendations of the round table. However the round table chose not to depose the city assembly, even though the election fraud of 1989 was no longer in dispute. Instead, it expressly tolerated the existence and the function of the assembly members for the short time until the new municipal elections.

In the Bible it says: "No one fills old wineskins with new wine." But the compromise of the transition was exactly that: for a while, the new content was to be conveyed within the old structures. Under the table, though, this meant that cuckoos from the bankrupt state, GDR, were able to place many an egg in the usual nests and, above all in the economy, see to it that their cuckoo offspring claimed good jobs for themselves. But the hopes and ideas that emerged from the *Neues Forum* movement and from other new forces were like new wine: not yet ready for use, not finished fermenting and maturing. Many wishes and well-intended proposals rose to the surface like bubbles and burst in the harsh air of reality.

What was the round table supposed to accomplish in Greifswald? Education, the school system, and recreational activities for young people and children – a working group, a so-called "little round table for education," presented its proposals and continued working even well after the new *Bürgerschaft* was in place.

Housing questions, the condition of older buildings, and the preservation of historical landmarks – a "working group: old city center" was formed, and it is still active today.

Advocating for the needs of the handicapped, a working group spoke up within the *Neues Forum*, and it still meets today – though now independently of the forum.

What did we want to move? The buildings of the old organizations were to be parceled out: the *SED* county offices, the GDR league of trade unions on *Rathenaustrasse*, the property of the Section for Military Medicine, the *Stasi* house at *Domstrasse* 7, the printery of the *Ostseezeitung* at the corner of *Bachstrasse* and *Löfflerstrasse*.

There is still a file folder, today, containing the many applications seeking to use or claiming to own the *SED* county office building. Its uses these days are rather varied. I recall, for example, a *CDU* party convention in this building at which a once-feared state official stood in the lobby selling technical literature for government administrators. It was noted aloud that the kindergarten formerly located at this address – a wooden barracks – had burned down very conveniently just in time to make room for the party's new building. It was proven that the multiple-stories-deep foundation, reinforced with pilings to withstand nuclear attack, was built illegally under special provisions for national defense. The *SED* did offer this building to the public in apparently direct fashion. Yet it has de facto remained the party headquarters of the *SED*, the *SED-PDS*, and now the *PDS*, and the question of ownership has since been decided in a way that does not correspond with the intentions of the round table.

The trade union building that housed the *FGDB* (*Freie deutsche*

Gewerkschafts-Bund) has dropped its "F" and is at the disposal of the *DGB* (*Deutsche Gewerkschafts-Bund*). One could write a political thriller about the property of the Military Medicine Section, whose main characters are the *SED* minister for national defense, Kessler, and his successor, the *CDU* minister for disarmament, Eppelmann. Among the beneficiaries are the former colonels of military medicine.

Amid the lively struggle back and forth, only the *Stasi* building at *Domstrasse* 7 was finally awarded to the university for its music students. Later it turned out that the round table had had no legal standing to do that. The decision remained in effect, although it then had to be legally protected by complicated means. And it was revoked anyway, because the *Bundesland* of *Mecklenburg-Vorpommern* arranged an exchange with itself. The university, which is operated by the *Bundesland*, received the rear building at *Domstrasse* 20 – the former county courthouse – for its music students. But the agencies of the *Bundesland*'s justice department were able to reclaim ownership of the original court building at *Domstrasse* 7. So here, too, the decision of the round table was not upheld in the end.

What was the round table meant to hinder? Real estate speculation. The decision of the round table was also confirmed by the city assembly, so that in the last months of the GDR, only those parcels of land could change hands where people had built their own homes and now owned houses situated on land that was still property of the state.

Further, the round table was intended to hinder corruption, avoid privileged treatment of functionaries, and prevent the allocation of leadership positions to *Stasi* people and other suspicious persons, and from case to case it was able to effectively lodge objections or even a veto.

In the few months between December 1989 and April 1990 the round table in Greifswald, as well as elsewhere, earned great respect and high recognition for its moral actions, for it stood as a guarantor for continuity in transition, for non-violent dialogue between old and new forces, an identity for the city's image of itself, and an uncorrupted starting point from which to evolve forward.

On Friday, May 4, Mayor Wellner invited the round table to a concluding session. On May 6, 1990 the first democratic, local elections took place. In this way, the duties and responsibilities of the round table ended.

Elections

1990 was the year of elections. For the first time since 1933, for the first time after twelve years of fascist dictatorship and forty-four years of socialist dictatorship, free and democratic elections were carried out – four elections: on March 18 for the *Volkskammer*, the national assembly of the GDR; on May 6, the local elections; on October 14, elections for the legislatures of the *Länder*; and on December 2, for the first time all Germany voted to elect the *Bundestag*. Thus the groundwork was laid for new, legitimate representation at the various levels. For until now, the elections had been a cross between a census and and a ritual bow of submission. The quotas for the *SED*, its satellite parties, and the socialist organizations had been fixed for decades at the levels of the 1948 elections. The composition of the unity lists was arranged under the table by the National Front. Only in the last years was it possible to cross off individual candidates from the ballots.

The local elections of May, 1989 showed for the first time greater accommodation to the people's wishes. I recall election gatherings in student dormitories, at which I was among the invited guests. There, in April 1989, the election and the way it was carried out were thoroughly discussed, including some official representations in which the election was compared to the counting of cattle. Then, in May, the counting of votes was carried out under the watchful eye of citizens. On the evening following those elections, I was able to compose a list of the election results for nineteen of the fifty-two polling places in Greifswald, since it was mainly a number of students who had collected the results. The results stood in clear contradiction to those that were published the next day. As I learned later, my repeated objection to the election was the only one made in Greifswald. There was no reaction, except that perhaps this is why, in the fall of 1989, my name appeared on the lists of those who would be interned in the new concentration camps. The projected date to start populating these camps was reportedly December 10, 1989. The *Wende* preempted that.

The peace services, the demonstration marches, the forums and the round table created a massive shift in the interplay of forces in society. Now, for the first time, elections following a free and democratic method would create clear legitimacy for the parties and their lists of candidates. The spectrum ran from *SED*, now re-named *PDS* (Party of Democratic Socialism), through a series of middle-class parties stretching from right to left, through other movements and groupings and on to the list of the Beer Drinkers, who evidently aimed to make fun of the elections but were allowed to participate anyway.

The market square in Greifswald testifies to the enthusiasm with which the elections of March 18 were prepared. Out of the Wednesday demonstrations, groups slowly evolved that would represent the new or the old parties. The centers around which they crystallized had established their political profiles and got the measure of each other at the round table. Above all, though, prominent figures from Bonn showed up as major campaigners. Former chancellor Willy Brandt (*SPD*) came, *CDU* general secretary Volker Rühe showed up. Again and again the Western campaigners prepared us for the new reality. They warned us against the great enemy: that was either the *CDU* if an *SPD* speaker was at the microphone, or it was the *SPD* if the *CDU* was hosting the event.

I still remember exactly how Volker Rühe told off a group of youthful and oppositional types who were disrupting the rally, saying that of course such relics of socialism as they were hadn't learned anything and of course they couldn't be real Greifswalder. The fact that all of us together had just got rid of the GDR-socialism of

Ulbricht and Honecker, of Mielke and Stoph, that our opponent was the *SED*, and that by means of the round table we had just fired the last official *Stasi* employee from *Domstrasse* 7 on February 28, just three weeks before . . . all that got little attention. No, it was clear who the new enemy was: the *CDU* for the *SPD* and vice versa. All as if there had never been an *SED*. And so the Federal Germans drove us against one another into the new future. A new polarization erupted, long before the issues themselves might have brought it about.

The *CDU* had a hard time, because for a long time the East-*CDU* was rejected by the West-*CDU*: no one wanted to have anything to do with the "wooden flute players" in the former satellite party of the *SED*. Actually, everyone in the GDR had been playing the same tune, and now each party – *SED*, *SPD*, or West-*CDU* – was trying to put the blame on someone else. So it came about that as late as February, a clear majority seemed to favor the *SPD*. But then, when the *CDU*, East and West, went on the offensive together, they quickly won a substantial majority, since the *Deutschmark*, the banana, and German unity seemed most likely to be had with them.

In the national legislative elections on March 18, it became clear that the Chancellor of the Federal Republic, Helmut Kohl, had won the election in the GDR. The *CDU* under Lothar de Mazière held by far the most seats and the presidency in the now democratically constituted People's Chamber and its new government.

The overwhelming victory of the *CDU* in March provided a sense of how the results of the local elections on May 6 might look. The *CDU* won in Greifswald as well. Since I had been the lead candidate for the *CDU*, my first steps early the next morning led me to the headquarters of the *SPD*, which were then in a dilapidated building on Wiesenstrasse. There, amid the socialist ruins of Greifswald, I found the speaker of the *SPD*, Herr Fuhrmann, and with him Herr Mirass, standing gloomily by the street, having come nowhere near the electoral victory they had hoped for. Even the *PDS* had more votes than they got. I wanted to show my solidarity with them and make it clear that we would all continue to work together for the good of the city of Greifswald. To this day, it is incomprehensible to me with what consistently bitter, inflammatory rhetoric the *SPD* caucus and its speaker, Thomas Fuhrmann, railed against the *CDU* and against me personally, to the detriment of the city itself: side by side with the *PDS*, and supported by the *Neues Forum*, they paralyzed the newly-created *Bürgerschaft* for nearly a year and a half. Apparently they had not been able to get over the fact that, in the entire GDR, the very pro-*SPD* mood had not led to the majority they had hoped for.

The election in the newly-constituted *Länder* on October 14 was another clear victory for the *CDU*. Only Brandenburg became a *Land* governed by *SPD*, and it seems to me that happened entirely because the well-known and well-respected administrative head of the Evangelical Church in Berlin-Brandenburg, Manfred Stolpe, was far more convincing than his *CDU* counterpart, Diestel, who after only a few months was aligned more closely with *PDS* chief Gysi than with his own party.

Naturally, as events in Germany and in the world led to reduced East-West tensions, the December 2 elections for the legislature of the united Germany led to a victory for the *CDU* and for its chancellor, Helmut Kohl, who had even come to Greifswald to campaign in person.

We, who had learned to be citizens of the GDR, had had to cope with, among other things, a total of six governments within scarcely fourteen months, from Erich Honecker by way of Egon Krenz and Hans Modrow, via Lothar de Maiziere to Helmut Kohl's existing government and, finally, his newly elected administration; and at the same time we had to deal with the demise of central state authority in the GDR and its ministries, the handing over of districts to district trustees, the creation of five *Länder* from scratch, the restructuring of national legislature and city charter, the change of currency, and the changeover of all laws from socialist jurisprudence to the legal system of the Federal Republic.

At the core of these changes were the elections. I can still see the packed polling places in March, when the votes were being counted. In December, the joy surrounding the elections was more temperate. But above all, the new parties found suitable personalities in short supply. Each party had to take, so to speak, anything that had legs and belonged to its camp and put them into the spots that needed filling, so that in the long run it was scarcely possible to do much party building at the grass-roots level.

And soon, it will be time for the next round: 1994 with four elections – local, *Länder*, national, and European Union elections.

I hope the citizens won't again be subjected to the schizophrenia that accompanied the last elections. Each citizen is represented at three levels by different representatives. The representatives to the *Bundestag* determine the laws at the federal level, that we are all subject to, but they are far removed from daily life in Greifswald. They unburden the federal government and don't feel responsible if those burdens fall to the *Land* or the local governments. While the representatives to the *Landtag* have to accept the federal laws, they can in turn shift a great deal of the burden to the local level, often without noticing what that means for the towns and cities. The members of the *Bürgerschaft* groan under the burdens heaped upon them by the *Bundestag* or *Landtag*, but they are subordinate to both and thus have no choice but to find a way to handle it all. Adequate communication among the representatives at the three levels does not take place. The *Ministerpräsidenten* at the head of their *Land* governments engage in a give and take with the *Bundestag* by way of their seats on the federal *Bundesrat*. But mayors and district administrators have to accept it as an act of grace if they get even a hearing before a committee of the *Landtag*. Only the parties assert their line at all three levels and control even the *Bundesrat*, which is actually supposed to represent the individual *Länder*.

I find that the recent discussion concerning regulations for political asylum-seekers offers a striking example of this schizophrenia. When flames roared at a hostel for asylum-seekers in Rostock-Lichtenhagen, the interior minister for the *Land* and, at the local level, the mayor had to face their responsibility. The years-long public tug of war over this issue among representatives in the *Bundestag*, which may have been the real cause of that riot, was scarcely mentioned. Yet in the *Bundestag*, ideology and party discipline took priority over the good of the country, dragged out the long-overdue resolution of this issue for years and, in the end, put the club and the Molotov cocktail into the hands of the radicals.

It is greatly to be wished that the parties again might place the good of the country and its citizens above their ideologies and their jockeying for position and power. Now, in the coming election campaign, again it will be the citizen who decides. One can only hope that the parties will do better at keeping their eyes on the greater good.

City Charter

Those were strange weeks, in late April and May, 1990. City assembly and round table ceased operations. Even before the election, representatives of *CDU*, *SPD* and *Neues Forum* sat down together and resolved to work together, preparing to administer the city. Above all, we puzzled together over a document that the German league of cities had sent us. It outlined five different frameworks for a municipal charter. These frameworks were patterned after the examples of the Western occupying forces, who, after 1945, had brought their own models to bear. Osnabrück, located in the formerly British occupation zone, has an English city charter with an unpaid chief mayor who is the de facto president of the city council and spokesperson for the city, and a chief city manager, elected to a twelve-year term, who, as a technocrat, is responsible for the entire administration. Herr Pösse and Herr Bouché came from the municipal administration of Osnabrück and helped us to develop the city charter for Greifswald following this model. The honorary chief mayor (*CDU*) would be supported by a city manager (*SPD*) in the sense that the latter would be responsible for administration. Thus the chief mayor was in charge of the city as a whole, but no agencies reported directly to him. His deputy, the first mayor, however, was in charge of the main office, personnel, legal, press, and a variety of other offices. This model was continued, even when, on May 17, right in the middle of these deliberations, the national assembly decided upon a municipal charter for the entire territory of the GDR, in which the chief mayor received primary responsibility for the entire administration. The role of city spokesperson would be shared with the president of the *Bürgerschaft*.

No later than 30 days after the local elections, the new municipal administration had to be in office. On May 29, the constitutive session of the new *Bürgerschaft* took place. The negotiations among the parties over the distribution of the various department head posts had continued until after midnight. The *SPD* was not able to propose a first mayor from Greifswald, but was pleased to have found a fellow Social Democrat from Hamburg to take the job.

So the day arrived for the first meeting of the *Bürgerschaft*. The auditorium of the university provided a solemn meeting place. Frau Flick, chief mayor of our partner city, Osnabrück, had come to witness this landmark event in Greifswald's history. The meeting was convened by the oldest representative, Herr Schneider. With overwhelming majorities, Dr. Thomas Meyer was elected president of the *Bürgerschaft*, and I was elected chief mayor. Thereupon we all got our first look at the candidate for the position of first mayor: Herr Kammradt, an *SPD* party manager from Hamburg, who had been of help as the new party constituted itself in Rostock. At that point, nothing was certain regarding the future re-unification of Germany. Thus, with his election as first mayor, Herr Kammradt also became a citizen of the Hanseatic City of Greifswald, and therefore also a citizen of the GDR. Given the fact that his family was still living in

Hamburg, this was a resolute step.

In the process of electing the senators, there were still open questions concerning the departments of finance and business. These were resolved in the course of the session, so that in the end the five remaining senators could be elected as well. Thus, the leadership of the administration was in place and authorized to begin its work. In my address as chief mayor, I announced my ideas and plans. After the close of the session, the newly-elected officials and their guests of honor moved to the Theatercafé, where a table had been reserved. In the city hall that afternoon, in the presence of the new senate, I disbanded the old city council and discharged its members. At the next meeting of the *Bürgerschaft*, the majority of the new officials were formally installed, so that the city administration was essentially complete.

At the same time, there were important tasks to perform. Those who had built their own homes wanted ownership of the property under those houses to be transferred to their names before the currency union, scheduled for July 1, went into effect. The budget had to be reviewed in preparation for the changeover to the *Deutschmark* and to a Western-style market economy. And a new determination was made via votes of confidence, as a result of which 19 of 21 school principals had to be replaced before summer vacation began.

With time, the discrepancies between the intentions behind Greifswald's city charter on the one hand, and the municipal charter (passed by the GDR national assembly) on the other, led, in the context of concrete events, to grave conflicts within the *Bürgerschaft* and the city's administration.

For one thing, the first mayor, as deputy of the chief mayor, had the most important strings of administration in his hands, but the responsibility for everything was given to the chief mayor. This discrepancy had serious effects, not least because positions occupied by *CDU* and *SPD* were facing off here, and the parties' own interests increasingly took priority over the needs of the city and its citizens. In addition, the *Neues Forum* in particular, but also the *SPD*, wanted to formulate resolutions for the senate to stand behind. However, for a city the size of Greifswald, the municipal charter placed the formulation of resolutions – and responsibility for the administration – exclusively in the hands of the chief mayor, so that the resolutions of the senate had only the character of recommendations. Although as a rule I adhered to the resolutions of the senate, this point led to severe discord on more than one occasion. Only gradually did I come to fully understand the position I found myself in, and for months the senate disputed my authority, contrary to all rules and laws. It took a year before the conflicts broke out openly and drove the partners in *Bürgerschaft* and senate against one another. It took only two years for the *Bürgerschaft* to reach complete paralysis. One attempt to amend the city charter had to do with the composition and authority of committees within the *Bürgerschaft*. Countless strained talks between the party caucuses consumed time and nerves. The result, however, failed in almost every case to reach the required two-thirds majority. A large part of the energy of the *Bürgerschaft* did not address the city's affairs, but was instead dissipated in senseless formal matters. In one matter, however, the necessary majority was achieved to amend the city charter. It was a matter of formulating a statute concerning the administration of neighborhoods for Wieck/Eldena and for Riemserort/Riems. But here the legal oversight board lodged an objection. Nevertheless, neighborhood mayors were able to be elected in both Wieck/Eldena and in Riemserort/Riems.

Die Bürgerschaft

With the elections on May 6, 1990, the relative strengths of the parties in Greifswald were fixed for the next four years. Eleven parties or groups were represented in the new *Bürgerschaft*. Soon, five factions were formed. BFD, *CDU*, DBD, DSU joined together and comprised the largest faction with twenty-seven representatives in all. The old ruling party, *SED*, now re-organized as *PDS*, remained the second-largest contingent with 13 seats, and they were supported by the faction of four women (DVD, the Greens, UFV, and VS – some of these women had once belonged to the *SED*). The third strongest faction was the newly-founded *SPD* with eleven representatives (among them was one of the four founding members of the new party, originally named SDP, Pastor Noack). And finally, the *Neues Forum* had five seats.

The original alliance during the *Wende* – the big faction, consisting of *CDU*, *SPD* and *Neues Forum* – assumed responsibility for the administration and provided the chief mayor and the six senators. Thus, forty-three representatives stood with their factions in support of the new administration, opposed by the seventeen seats of the *PDS* and the womens' faction. From the outset, the city's representative assembly called itself *Bürgerschaft*, following Hanseatic tradition.

At the sessions of the *Bürgerschaft*, one speaker from the *PDS* soon emerged, who as a former *SED* comrade had now become a guardian of democracy and carped with unfailing regularity about matters of form and procedure. On very many issues, members of the same faction voted differently. So far, the *Bürgerschaft* was showing no understanding of – and no confidence in – the work of its own committees. So the *Bürgerschaft* behaved like one big committee, and its discussions of principles and information often extended until midnight and beyond. The uncertainty in this business, which was understandable and to be expected, and an unstoppable tendency to revisit fundamental questions, gave outsiders an impression that was harmful for the *Bürgerschaft*, which was mockingly compared with a theater or a kindergarten. To me, this seemed an unavoidable phase – democracy passing through its adolescence.

It turned out to be a great hindrance to our work within the *Bürgerschaft* and the administration, that during the transition period – from GDR-socialism to democratic GDR, then to joining the Federal

Republic and the European Union – that during this prolonged period, the basis of law, the jurisdictive, was extremely uncertain. To that extent it must be seen and duly acknowledged that, on the one hand, the representatives went about their tasks with great seriousness and energy, and that, on the other hand, in a time of profound changes and the absence of legal foundations, they were constantly forced to work out a basic understanding of what they were doing.

Naturally, the points of departure for such a basic understanding varied. And so on the part of the comrades from *PDS* and *SPD* there was a tendency toward planned economy, maintenance of community ownership of property, and a kind of communal socialism, which found forceful advocates among the members of *Neues Forum* and the women's faction. But also within the big faction, the attitude toward privatization of what had been "property of the people" was restrained, out of habit and in the face of the many competing interests. In *Neues Forum* there was strong support for ecological issues, resistance against the new role of money and, of course, a tendency toward grassroots democracy. Even in the big faction, it was only slowly and with great effort, including partial agreement from the *PDS*, that the realization gained acceptance that the city's budget could not be overloaded with expenditures, and not just because the municipal charter said it couldn't. Given the economic collapse, the fundamental re-structuring and the massive pent-up demand, such a realization was by no means a matter of course, especially since the yardstick for our desires and for our legal demands was the constantly visible standard set by the old Federal Republic.

Since the so-called coalition agreement between the big faction, *SPD* and *Neues Forum* in May, 1990, had not been finally set down in writing – the time pressure had simply been far too great – in 1991 there were protracted, time-consuming efforts (which also increased the friction among the parties) to reach such a written coalition agreement. The unsurprising result came in January, 1992: the coalition failed, with each former partner blaming the others. For months there was a stalemate between the chief mayor and the big faction versus a unified majority in the opposition totaling 35 votes. This stalemate was determined increasingly by the interests of the political parties, and it did great harm to the Hanseatic City of Greifswald.

The municipal charter assumed that an elected representative could keep his seat and his vote, even if he were elected to serve as a senator and administrative director. Under the impression that the separation of legislative and executive powers is meaningful and necessary, those senators who had been elected to the *Bürgerschaft* gave up their seats in that body. Only the chief mayor retained his seat and his vote, because this had been prescribed in the municipal charter. This practice of relinquishing one's seat applied to three senators from the *CDU* and one senator of *Neues Forum*. The two *SPD* senators had not been elected to the *Bürgerschaft* anyway. But these were not the only votes that had to be replaced within the *Bürgerschaft*. Over the months, many members left, either because they had moved away from Greifswald, or because as entrepreneurs they didn't want to risk the appearance of a conflict of interest. Others left because they could no longer devote the time and energy required by so many demands. Some members accepted assignments in Schwerin or in Bonn and had to relinquish their seats for that reason. After only two and a half years, twenty-four of the sixty seats were occupied by successors to the original members.

Of course there were special interests represented in the *Bürgerschaft*, including, for example, those of individual neighborhoods within the city. Thus the departure of the BFD members from the big coalition can be traced back to the situation in Riems.

The public also played a not insubstantial role in determining the course of events at the *Bürgerschaft*. Audience members often came to support or oppose specific measures, and through individual representatives, factions, or even by means of conversations during recesses, they exercised influence over the course of its sessions.

Occasionally, that influence was reinforced by demonstrations by interest groups. Sometimes, the employees of kindergartens and daycare facilities would speak out and hold up a session; sports clubs, schoolchildren and their teachers, the handicapped, workers from the island of Riems also made themselves heard loud and clear. The *Bürgerschaft* assembly hall was taken over at times by kindergarten employees, and the mayor's office by upset young people. Outside the door of the city hall there were many demonstrations. On February 15, 1991 alone, there were three demonstrations: the kindergarten workers brought children from their groups and filled the assembly hall, foyer and stairwell of the city hall as the *Bürgerschaft* was scheduled to meet; a demonstration opposing the Gulf War, which was just beginning, marched to the city hall and began a discussion in the city hall foyer, and a third group stood in the hallway outside the chief mayor's office and presented its demands.

During the early period, as we moved from dictatorship toward democracy, the *Bürgerschaft* had adhered strictly to the principle of separation of powers and saw itself as a smaller version of parliament, or of the *Bundestag*. Only slowly did the administration and the *Bürgerschaft* come to understand that the separation of powers isn't so strictly applied in a democracy on the local level, and that, in practice, a greater sharing of decision-making and responsibility turns out to be realistic – and that such sharing is anticipated in the municipal charter. To that extent, the basic roles of government and opposition were exaggerated, and now they will have to find their right proportion in response to actual conditions within the community, i.e. the Hanseatic City of Greifswald and its inhabitants.

City Administration

In the GDR era, there were two hundred forty employees in the Greifswald city hall. The administration could get by with this small number, because most decisions were made outside the city hall anyway, namely in the *SED* and in the central government in Berlin or at the district level in Rostock. The city was a low-level administrative unit bound to instructions from above. There was little local self-administration to be seen, only certain accents could be set, based on knowledge of local circumstances. Few of the state-owned plants were under the control of city administration; they included, for example, the slaughterhouse, the state-owned lumber yard, and the housing administration. The essential operations were under the authority of the district (electronic communications), and/or national government (nuclear power plant).

Of the fifteen members of the old city council, we wanted to keep only four, and those only as department heads. Today only one of them remains in a city office. Once there was an assembly to address questions of food supply for the city. The responsible people were quickly called together: the mass retail outlets *HO* and *Konsum* and the wholesalers. The former department for trade and logistics was about to be dissolved, however. The new problem was waste disposal, and questions of street cleaning, garbage removal and landfills were among the first provisions that had to be put in place afresh. Questions of ownership had to be cleared up immediately. The old provision, that there was ownership by the people as a whole with the attendant legal structure, had to be cleared up in two directions. On the one hand, applications for purchase, lease, rent, or compensation were piling up by the hundreds. On the other, the city was required, between June 20 and September 20, to inventory all property it originally owned.

We wanted to replace the GDR's central administration as soon and as comprehensively as possible with local self-administration. Policies and regulations for the transition reached us from the GDR government and from district administration, as well as recommendations from the (West German) federal government and even the League of German Cities. Our partner city, Osnabrück, also helped, providing administrative assistants, training courses, consultants and office supplies.

Only, it was often impossible to get the information we needed. In the beginning, telephone connections were very difficult to make and took an inordinate amount of time. Printed material, even from Berlin, arrived weeks late. Very many messages we had to send by courier, and often we had to make do with less-than-admissable, legally valid documents. Even working in-house was difficult. The best way to make a copy was with carbon paper and a typewriter. The few jobs we could produce in larger numbers quickly filled the offices with the alcohol smell of mimeograph ink. In the months that followed, generous support from Osnabrück has seen to it that our paperwork is now done with the aid of modern technology, including a network of computers, copiers, and fax machines. However, what we once believed to be the unbearable burden of bureaucracy in GDR times has now turned to a nostalgic dream, for in evident contradiction to the data protection required today, all the registrations and checklists, application forms, rules notices, and legal entitlements have bound us into a continuous cycle of stress under the new bureaucracy. If one compares the typical 20cm x 1cm open pay slip from GDR days with the sealed Din A5 (14.8cm x 21cm) pay envelopes today, one has an idea of how much the paperwork load has increased.

In the process, of course, many procedures were stood on their heads, or taken from upside-down and stood on their feet. The same real estate office employees who had spent decades carrying out expropriation of private properties and their re-assignment into "property of the people" now encountered those same homeowners and their applications for restitution, return, re-purchase, and privatization. While there was more money than goods under socialism, and more jobs than workers, here too everything is reversed: more goods than money, more people seeking work than there are jobs. Government offices spend their time dealing with removal rather than supply, with job cuts rather than job creation. Administrative procedures are similarly reversed, which causes complicated adjustments. At the cemetery in Annaberg, residents point out a linden tree. It was supposedly planted with its limbs in the ground, and since then, the roots have produced the leaves. I have often been reminded of that linden tree.

The first of January, 1991 hit the new administration like a hammer. On this day, we inherited the legacy of the GDR's ministries. What had been administered and paid for in Berlin, or through district authorities in Rostock, was now the city's business. All kindergartens, child care services, school administration, many sports facilities, the professional fire departments, registration of residents, automobile registrations and the like – were all now the responsibility of the city. All the public clinics and the health system at factories and businesses disappeared into a void without a legal successor. From the 240 employees at the city hall, we suddenly jumped to 3,000, who, with all their duties, rights and needs, were now allocated to the chief mayor as their new employer. Most of their jobs are public and heavily subsidized. This had helped cause the bankruptcy and collapse of socialism. Now the city was supposed to assume responsibility for those tasks and burdens.

Assistance from the federal government and from the *Land* were understood to be transitional, and it was reduced within a very short time. Thus, with this day there began an endless chain of efficiency and savings measures, hundreds of job cuts, and the whole gamut of dances with personnel council and unions, with court dates and settlements. With enthusiasm we had signed on to build up, but, brutally sobered, we were forced instead to tear down. As of 1993, 1,700 people work within the framework of city administration, but still further reductions will be necessary. For the personnel costs in the city budget can't be allowed to restrict the administration's flexibility completely.

This wasn't the problem in the begining, because the salaries were fixed at 35% of comparable West German income. But if the increase and incremental equalization with the West German standard is to happen in great leaps – to 60%, 70%, 74%, 84%, and finally 100% – then alongside the joy of the earners there will be the shock of the newly unemployed, and the worry on the other side about how such a sudden salary increase, of 25% for example, can be paid for. Of course, it also made an impression when assistants and consultants and colleagues who came to us from the old *Bundesländer* – and who continue to do so – naturally keep earning at 100%. At times, the additional, tax-exempt, so-called hardship bonuses of the assistants were greater than the gross income of their superiors. But on this subject there was surprisingly little agitation and grumbling.

What was agitating, though, was the lack of orientation. For GDR regulations expired, one after the other, and federal German legislation, in all its confusing interface with the unification treaty, had to be first understood and then put in place. By-laws of the *Bürgerschaft* took months, even years, before they were available to be implemented, and the same was true for the laws of the *Land*, since the *Land Mecklenburg-Vorpommern* was just now taking shape, after the local administrations had already been at work for half a year. Thus, the task at hand was not just to consider, to learn and to practice, but also to take on a great deal of risk for decisions that already are being measured against the implacable standard of West German law and placed into the merciless web of interests guarded by well-paid attorneys. It also has a substantial effect that, more and more, collective thinking is being supplanted by the demands of individuals and groups in conflict with one another, so that a normal procedure turns into a tug of war or a test of wills.

We still don't have a good handle on the transition of affairs from the domain of government agencies to independent operations, associations or corporations, the transition from senators to members of supervisory boards, or from chief mayor to shareholder in housing administration, public utilities, or professional associations. And what checks and balances should apply to community property, between society at large and the *Bürgerschaft?*

So it was not long before one could sense, around the senate table, which party was trying to have its say by way of its senator, and soon disagreements broke out that drove the city and the county into frustrating antagonism – and a merry game of pass-the-buck flourished between *Land* government and city administration.

Should one consider it a relaxation of the tense atmosphere that every employee has submitted his or her statement concerning past cooperation with the *Stasi*, but the Gauck board[9] has only just now released its criteria for evaluating those statements? Thus, an orderly screening of the personnel has not yet been possible. Thus, many an employee has built his nest on a branch, while it has yet to be determined how sturdy that branch will be.

One problem awaits attention: the city administration is distributed among nineteen buildings. But when there is discussion of erecting one new administrative office building, a "technical" city hall, for the sake of efficiency and to save money, then right away every man and woman in the city is puzzled and upset at our strange set of priorities.

A Single Currency

In the summer of 1990, there were still two German states, and it was still an open question whether, and how, a single, unified German state might come about. Nevertheless, the Federal Republic of Germany and the now-democratic GDR under de Maizière decided to share a single economy and a single currency. On July 1, 1990, GDR money became invalid, and the longed-for *Deutschmark* made its triumphant entrance. All citizens of the GDR, including children, could receive up to DM 4,000 at an exchange rate of 1:1; after that, it was two GDR marks for one *Deutschmark*. Both assets and debts were calculated on this basis.

---

[9] Former Rostock pastor and *Neues Forum* spokesman Joachim Gauck headed the German government agency charged with archiving and evaluating the enormous number of files left behind by the *Stasi*, and determining rules for their use. In 2012, Gauck was elected Federal President of Germany.

Back when endless lines of Trabbis were pouring across the border in November and December, 1989, almost everyone had picked up his or her DM100 "welcome money" to get a first whiff of the new atmosphere. Also, in advance of the re-valuation of all GDR currency values, the terrain was prepared on all sides by means of legal or illegal transactions on accounts, by means of purchases, by holding back invoices and goods, in West German exchange shops or even by way of Polish currency artists who did magic tricks with zero to infinity *Zloty*. It was not only at Berlin's Zoo train station that black marketeers stood on the streetcorner with their hands and pockets full of banknotes.

The newly-established city administration with its agencies and departments, some of which did not yet have their new staff in place, felt the storm front of the currency union passing overhead. One of the consequences it left in its wake was that the budget year was split in two. One set of books for the first half of 1990 had to be closed and balances figured in GDR currency. For the second half of 1990, from July 1 through December 31, in the end only a general accounting was required, containing above all a confirmation that no monies had been embezzled. With regular administrative funds under every heading, with subsidies, special allocations, and grants from the coffers of the GDR, the district, the federal government, the European Community, the *Land*, with failed or successful applications or even without them, finances in Greifswald – and not only in Greifswald – experienced much the same thing water does in a washing machine.

In the city, as in other places, the first signs quickly appeared that the currency of the GDR, with all its levels of deception, had disappeared. People said of it, you never know whether it's really money, vouchers, or just colored paper. Hard currency, the *Deutschmark*, had now taken its place, and it has been hard on us. It offers a firm footing for those that have it. Those that don't – they fall into a deep hole.

The first ones to notice that fact were the few remaining private businesses, but the many state-owned ones did, too. Their capital (as well as their credits and debts) was reduced by 50% on July 1. At the same time, they were still supposed to come up with wages, salaries, expenses, and purchases at 100%. Above all, it was the last, brave small business owners, who had fought their way through all of socialism, who now faced almost insurmountable problems. Just imagine, for comparison's sake, a solid, West German company – and then cut its capital in half. What would probably happen?

What did happen, however, came primarily from the outside. From that hour on, traditional trade partners from the former Soviet bloc and the Comecon zone were unable to pay for any goods. For GDR-Marks, there were well-established ways to handle transactions. But now, suddenly, there was hard currency to deal with. They didn't have it, and thus they were no longer potential customers. Across the GDR, this meant the loss of about one third of sales, which simply no longer existed. Even the support of West German credits and guarantees was unable to stabilize the collapsing trade situation with the countries of Eastern Europe.

What was left for our local producers was the Western market. But only a few had the means of production they would need to compete with the right quality and at the right price in the already-saturated European Community market. So the hopes of many turned to the former domestic GDR market. But here the street vendors, chain stores and used car dealerships invaded like a swarm of locusts, and the old GDR customer base was hungry for Western products. Even fish, eggs, butter and cheese were brought from Holland as far as the market in Greifswald. And of course, an egg from a refrigerated warehouse in the West was far superior to an egg from even the best GDR poultry farm. Full of euphoria, everyone first ate their fill of the new products. Bananas were the biggest hit, or for a while it was yogurt in plastic cups.

In the midst of wonderful summer weather, an oriental bazaar unfolded on the market square. I will never forget how Greifswalders turned into magical Aladdins, strolling through the market across a sea of carpets that had been laid out for sale. In the blink of an eye, the new cash disappeared into the pockets of the West Germans, who could now trade in their used cars for new ones. In the end, the GDR stores *Konsum* and *HO* were taken over by chains that had set contracts with their suppliers and, naturally, found no room for products from the GDR on their shelves. And the many kilometers of additional transportation costs had to be figured in, so that we here in *Vorpommern* were facing prices up to 150% of the West German norm. This led the city administration to undertake great efforts, for the sake of competition, to attract a discount market to Greifswald as quickly as possible.

Thus, the producers in the GDR were as good as shut down on the day the currency unified: they had no market in the East, no market in the West, and no market at home. What they had left was 50% of their savings, credits, and their determination not to give up – and a production plant that was soon graced with a new name: GDR legacy site. Accordingly, at the end of 1991, instead of the roughly 40 million marks that a West German city of similar size could expect in business tax income for the year, the city administration of Greifswald had taken in only three million marks.

Most of us did not become aware of this catastrophe right away. How many of us drove to Lübeck, Hamburg, Berlin or Osnabrück to do our shopping! How few made a point of buying local products! How few producers shifted their emphasis to sales in order to get their own products off their hands! When we, of the city administration, tried to set up a Pomerania market for farms in the region, it was not accepted. Just occasionally, a truck from one of the large collective farms would pull up at the market with vegetables and potatoes for sale.

No, Western goods with their colorful packaging and their mass supply crowded their way to the front of the shelf and the front of people's minds. Even the flowers at the market carried the quality emblem of Western magnificence and omnipresence. Fruit and vegetables appeared in *Vorpommern*, polished and shined like they were going to a wedding. The *Wende* was visible even in little mom and pop shops, where they still existed: milk and other beverages were no longer available in bottles; instead, they came in packages. Many kinds of breakfast rolls were on display. Shelf upon shelf of cleaning and washing products were taken down and replaced. Sausage shrink-wrapped in plastic, and a huge number of new varieties of cheese provided for uncertainty and disrupted the rhythms of habits built up over decades. What else were we supposed to buy? And who can blame us for switching like that? Every one of us recalls, for example, the pre-Christmas ritual, when people stood in long lines outside *HO* and *Konsum* waiting for their bag with the allotted two oranges per person per year. Now hard currency had come to us, with all its glory and its misery.

The Day of German Unity

Among many disturbing questions in the months of 1990, one stood out. With the German-German and international discussions, with the two-plus-four negotiations, will German unification be achieved? In August, the first projected dates were heard: September 14, October 10. With a clear intent to end its own existence, the GDR government worked toward the dissolution of the GDR and the transition to the unification of the two states. Early on it became clear that there would not be a new, shared constitution according to article 146; rather, incorporation into the existing Federal Republic according to article 23 of the Basic Law instead. Finally, October 3, 1990 was set as the Day of German Unity.

In the last days of September, the ministries of the GDR dissolved. Our proposed communal property inventories were supposed to be in Berlin by September 20. With great effort, we had managed to submit the lists punctually. Some of them came back by return mail, and the rest were lost in the mass of paper at the dissolved ministries. Also in September, 1990, the head of the trustee organization, Dr. Detlef Rohwedder, came to Greifswald, in order to speak with the chief mayors and county executives of the three northern districts of Schwerin, Rostock, and Neubrandenburg. I can still see him eating lunch with me in the *Ratskeller*, with his four bodyguards distributed around the room. It was the first time that he had left Berlin and traveled through territory of the GDR. I was too inexperienced to grasp the great danger under which he lived – and to which he fell victim a short time later. To us county executives and chief mayors, he spoke of the effort it took to get 100 telephone lines installed at his headquarters; it weighed upon him as well that the applications and petitions were piling up in his offices.

Back then, many people, with their unclear notions, worked hard to get rulings and contracts in order under GDR law; others postponed signing anything until federal German law was in effect. Since the fall of the wall, we had grown used to the idea of German unification. Now it was upon us *de jure* as well. But in practice, that became the essential point and content of this day: the GDR disappeared, and the rights and legal principles of the Federal Republic of Germany, and all the traditions upon which they rested, went into effect.

No one had had great respect for the class justice of the GDR, nor for the notaries, judges, lawyers and state's attorneys operating in this part of Germany. The bottom line, that the legal system had to serve the ruling class, led not only to legal uncertainty and prejudicial rulings based on party, but also to severe injustice. Like the legal system in the Nazi era, the GDR's legal system allowed itself to be misused as the party's henchman. Anyone who did not want to let himself be abused had great difficulties and little chance of success. But the methods of many a state's attorney could easily be compared with those of the infamous Nazi judge, Roland Freisler. Therefore, one of the demands of the *Wende* was that the fundamentally unjust system in place under the GDR and its party-based cadre structure be replaced. It is a liberating feeling to know that this system of injustice and a substantial number of its participants have been removed.

Nevertheless, on October 3, a situation was created that was difficult to bear. Even the relatively neutral legal proceedings of daily life were disrupted. The system of justice we had known was extinguished, the legal situation practically unsustainable. The remaining attorneys had to make fundamental changes, and to work out the many profound differences in detail. The new legal system went into effect immediately, but it was largely unfamiliar to us. True, we still had no way of knowing how thoroughly and how intensively it would affect our operations. And yet, decisions had to be made and answered for. Life went on, and it demanded many fundamental changes in how we did things.

In the spring of 1990 I had met Professor Günther Krause at a conference in Rostock. This neighbor from *Mecklenburg* had been working with others to develop additional rulings that would enable the transition from one legal system to another. The unification treaty had been drawn up quickly. In several areas, it is insufficient and inconsistent. To this day it is a problematic aid, sometimes easing the transition for Greifswald's administrators, but sometimes making their lives uncertain and more difficult. Yet this was the only way to achieve unity. And that gain is the one that counts.

With the new legal system, the Federal German establishment took control in what had been the GDR. The ideals and the cultural, ecological, moral, and ethical conceptions of the GDR era, the ideas of the *Wende*, of the intellectuals and of the *Neues Forum* receded again into the background. The law of the land now was West German law as expounded by its West German interpreters. It took us at city hall a while, too, to understand that nothing would hold up that wasn't based on current law. Whether the rulings are made in city administration, in the schools, in businesses, in the churches, or at the police, they are all measured by the yardstick of Federal German law with all its ramifications as it stands in the 1990s. Had it been imposed on us at its beginning, in the 1950s, for example, we would have been able to live with it. What we got just made the already complicated situation that much more complicated.

Summum ius summua iniuria – justice carried to its logical extreme can be profoundly unjust. We encounter this truth on many sides, especially in the small print and in things that are incomprehensible to the man on the street. At the city hall, many a well-intentioned ordinance, many a sensible resolution by the *Bürgerschaft*, had to be re-examined by the legal affairs office and, in the end, corrected. Finally, every last employee realized that agreements, and contracts in particular, had to be worked out by the legal affairs office – or at least signed off on by them. That is a huge imposition, especially since it turned out to be very difficult to attract good attorneys familiar with Federal German law to remote Greifswald at the not especially well-paying level of municipal administration. And so, for example, after we advertised for several positions and had fifty applicants, in the end only one attorney actually accepted our job offer. As a result, the demands on the legal affairs office and on the attorneys in city hall are very great. But that is the case everywhere. Attorneys in private practice are also getting plenty of work.

The needs of the university have become especially great. In 1945, the Soviet administration had closed the faculty of law at the Greifswald University "for all time". In a stroke of bravura, the rector and the directors of the university managed to re-open the faculty of law again in 1989-90 and have it blossom again as a vibrant branch, free of historical burdens, on the ancient tree of the alma mater. The new professors and lecturers that appeared in Greifswald, both as guests and in more permanent positions, have often been able to assist the city administration with advice and instruction about the law. In the end, the *Land* government decided to locate important courts in Greifswald: the fiscal court, the higher administrative court, the administrative court, and of course the district court for the area surrounding Greifswald itself. I had a chance to meet the first minister of justice of the *Land Mecklenburg-Vorpommern* even before he took office, during a visit to our church's partner congregation in Aegidienberg. So we had few difficulties understanding each other when it was time to decide where the courts would be housed. As we took a first walk through the city making a list of possible sites, Herr Haussmanns, president of the appellate court of *Mecklenburg-Vorpommern*, pointed out that, in the GDR, courts had been crowded into back buildings, and the imposing court buildings of an earlier age had often been allocated to the *Stasi*. And that's how it had been in Greifswald as well. The county court had vegetated at *Domstraße 20* in a back building well on its way to physical collapse, while the university section of Marxism/Leninism took residence in the front building. And in the old municipal court building at *Domstraße 7*, the *Stasi* had made itself at home. In the future, that picture will be set right again.

The Day of German Unity brought much good to us, who had learned to be citizens of the GDR. But it also pulled away the rug we had been standing on thus far, and it set us on the unfamiliar ground of solid, accumulated civil law. In the meantime, we have had to lay down our familiar and cherished desires, beliefs and principles at the altar of the new god. The Federal German legal system with all its implications makes one thing clear: on this throne sits the new central concept: 'ownership'.

It may not be beside the point to note here that on October 3, 1990, all of the so-called "property of the people" in the GDR, to the extent that it was assigned to the government or to the districts, passed into the hands of twelve West German persons, who are to dispose of it in accordance with federal financial interests: the commissioners of the *Treuhand*.

This fact is not the main point of the formal address that *Bürgerschaft* President Dr. Thomas Meyer gave in Greifswald in celebration of the Day of National Unity on October 3, 1990. But it has turned out to be the essential content of that date, determining the lives of former GDR citizens to an ever-increasing extent.

Vorpommern

"Maikäfer flieg! Dein Vater ist im Krieg. Deine Mutter ist im Pommerland,
Pommerland ist abgebrannt. Maikäfer flieg!"
Ladybug fly! Your father's in the war. Your mother's in Pomerania,
Pomerania is all burned down. Ladybug fly!
[-- a children's rhyme recalling the devastation of the Thirty Years'
War, 1618-1648.]

In the years from 1952 to 1954 I studied in Greifswald and began to
put down roots in *Vorpommern*. I immediately felt at home in this
region and its beautiful lowlands by the sea. I got to know the region
from the water and by land, and I was taken with its beauty. I recall
one day on the grounds of the convent Eldena, the ladybugs were
buzzing among the trees in mighty swarms, and you could shake
hundreds of them from a single branch. There are no more ladybugs
now. I saw a last single, crippled specimen of these scuttling bugs
years ago. But the people of *Vorpommern* have been through harsh
times as well. After the war, almost half the population was from
Hinterpommern. A substantial number of Greifswald's inhabitants had
fled or been driven out of Stettin (now Sczcecin, Poland). All these
people had had to begin again from scratch, without any
compensation, after all they owned had been lost in the war.

As Pomeranians they belonged to Prussia. Although Prussia
had already been absorbed into Greater Germany during the Third
Reich, the Allied Control Council decided it should be dissolved
again. The occupying forces created a *Land Mecklenburg* with a
goverment seat in Schwerin. The word *Pommern* was erased from the
map. Whoever used it was considered a *revanchist* and could be
punished accordingly.

In 1952 the *Länder* were dissolved. Districts were created.
Vorpommern was broken up into the districts of Rostock,
Neubrandenburg and Frankfurt/Oder. Under the centrally organized

leadership of the GDR the entire land became an open pantry for the capital, East Berlin. The district seats, in turn, could help themselves to whatever lay within their districts. The five year plans were the menu, so to speak. Everything was named and divided up nice and evenly. But they didn't all eat together. No, Berlin ate first, then the district seats, and only then did the rest of the hungry ones come to the table, and the tune was always the same: "If you come to dinner late, all you get is the scraps." *Vorpommern* had lost its regional center, Stettin. The *Mecklenburg* district seats of Rostock and Neubrandenburg helped themselves. In 1989 there were in all of *Mecklenburg* no cities that were as neglected and dilapidated as the *Vorpommern* cities of Stralsund and Greifswald. In 1945, Greifswald had been surrendered to the Red Army, undamaged by the war. After forty years of socialism, whole sections of the city lay in ruins, and when whole city blocks had to be razed, pre-fabricated apartment buildings would take their place. Three more years of socialism, and Greifswald's university, too, would have had to close – and send its students to Rostock.

If the *Wende* now offered us a new chance, how was it to be used?

The path forward for *Vorpommern* can be read on the map. In the 19th century, the economy grew up parallel to the Oder River. Two regularly used rail lines ran from Berlin to Stralsund. These transport lines continued from Stralsund via Sassnitz to Trelleborg in Sweden. The port of Mukran adjacent to Sassnitz reinforced this head of the economic axis that ran from Sweden through Stralsund, Berlin, Dresden, Prague, Bratislava, to Vienna and Budapest: a single economic strand that included four European capitals. This economic axis had been severed by the policy under socialism of isolating borders and erecting walls; it had disappeared from the minds of business leaders. With its *Autobahn* to Rostock, the GDR had shifted that axis to the west. In addition, *Vorpommern* itself was chopped up by district boundaries. For in Rostock, no one gave any thought to the lands south of the Peene River. And in

Neubrandenburg, thinking extended no farther than Anklam. After the *Wende,* the first measures to promote German unity focused on expanding east-west lines. We couldn't expect to find a sympathetic ear for our north-south economic axis anywhere. *Vorpommern* was all burned down. But our economic axis must be revived. That's where the emphasis should be put; the equally necessary east-west connection would come about anyway.

If we wanted to make use of this opportunity, people had to be mobilized. To this end, I sat down with Winfried Jax, the pastor in Stralsund. The two of us put out a flyer: "We are *Vorpommern,* not the backyard of *Mecklenburg*" was our rallying cry. We should be talking to Berlin and not to Schwerin, we are on the economic axis Sweden – Berlin. These were our main points. With this flyer we announced the first pro-*Vorpommern* demonstration, in Stralsund, on February 3, 1990. Many pastors' offices helped us to circulate these flyers. About 2,500 people – according to police estimates – walked in the February 3 demonstration from the railroad station to the square in front of city hall. For the first time in quite a few decades there were blue and white flags, and the red griffin (from the traditional Pomeranian crest) was raised. "*Vorpommern – Pommern vor*" the crowd chanted. Following the demonstration, a number of prominent people had been invited to gather in the rooms of the *Heiliggeistkirche.* A working group was formed, which soon was succeeded by the *Landesverband Vorpommern e. V.* After the municipal elections, many members of this new organization took on new functions. Thus, many of the group's initiatives were taken up by the same people as they served on the Council of Counties and Cities of *Vorpommern,* e.V., which met for the first time in the Greifswald city hall on June 28, 1990.

What were our aims? With the economic axis in mind, we argued for autonomy and the authority for *Vorpommern* to decide some matters on its own. Under no circumstances did we want Rostock or Neubrandenburg to continue deciding things over our heads. As much as possible, administration for our region should originate in *Vorpommern.* The *Autobahn* from Berlin to Stettin needs to be extended and expanded from Prenzlau to the area around Stralsund, with a smooth connection to Sassnitz and Mukran. The rail connection between Sassnitz and Stralsund needs to be fortified, and the ports of Sassnitz and Mukran are in need of a corresponding expansion. We further hoped and aimed to see the government subsidies for what had been East/West German border areas now be shifted to include the area along the Oder River. A Euro-Region that transcended national boundaries would have to promote and strengthen cooperation with the *Województwo*, or district, of Szczecin. In fact, *Vorpommern* would have to become a region in itself within the framework of the European Economic Community [which was officially succeeded by the European Union in December 1993]. Traditional links with the south of Sweden should be re-established and expanded. Without an identity as *Vorpommern*, these aims could not be realized. For this reason, *Vorpommern* must stand as a unit within the *Land*, able to speak for itself and represent its own interests. If these aims are not achieved, there will be no equal opportunity in Germany for the population of *Vorpommern*.

This was the scenario we started with in our efforts to help the people of *Vorpommern* emerge from their status quo of severe neglect. After the demonstration on February 3, 1990, Pastor Jax dropped out of this effort. But with a great deal of selfless energy, local knowledge, and political sensitivity, Siegwart Schmidt of Greifswald set to work on these matters. He became the first secretary of the *Landesverband Vorpommern*, the Council of Counties and Cities for *Vorpommern*. Following my election as mayor of the Hanseatic City of Greifswald, I was in a position to be elected chair of the Council of Counties and Cities, and as such I was able to take in hand many activities on behalf of *Vorpommern*.

Vorpommern as its own *Land* was one of the ideas in our heads that we needed to evaluate. Over many discussions and inquiries we had to set that idea aside and acknowledge that such a small *Land* could not survive. And so the question was: do we belong to Berlin-Brandenburg or to *Mecklenburg*? Berlin-Brandenburg would be our partner in terms of historical tradition, and from a business perspective as well. It would mean the natural and historically proven inclusion of our region in the North-South axis. What had once been the oldest Prussian university, in Greifswald, would be the only one in the *Land* of Brandenburg. The ports of Stralsund, Wolgast, Sassnitz and Mukran would be the *Land*'s only links to commerce by sea. Also, Berlin-Brandenburg would have need of what we have: land and water for recreation, agricultural products, and – we thought back then – energy from the atomic power plant in Lubmin on the outskirts of Greifswald. And Berlin-Brandenburg, on the other hand, has what *Vorpommern* needs: industrial products. *Mecklenburg*, by contrast, has traditions and a frame of mind that are oriented more toward Lübeck and Hamburg, and in many ways it competes directly with *Vorpommern*.

Before we were able to process all these considerations and begin to advocate for them in this new age of democracy, a *Land Mecklenburg-Vorpommern* was drawn over our heads, because the occupying powers had established such a *Land* in 1945. The matter was thus decided elsewhere, against our efforts and without consulting us – perhaps because a *Land* of *Mecklenburg* without *Vorpommern* isn't sustainable either.

If we were to belong to the *Land* of *Mecklenburg* now, our job was to limit the damage as much as possible. First, we focused on making sure the new *Land* got the double name *Mecklenburg-Vorpommern*. We owe it to the efforts of our representatives in the *Landtag* that the constitution refers to sections of the *Land*, and thus that *Vorpommern* has an identity that must be respected by law. The next question concerned the location of the *Land*'s capital city. A capital in *Vorpommern* was out of the question; the centrally located Güstrow was scarcely mentioned either. In the competition between Rostock and Schwerin, the Greifswald *Bürgerschaft* endorsed Rostock the day a delegation arrived to invite them to visit Schwerin. At a meeting with the *Landesverband Vorpommern* in the meeting room of the Protestant church council, Dr. Diederich, the future Minister of

Internal Affairs, made the case for Schwerin, citing common interests – but he was unable to persuade us. My answer was that this shared interest looked like the interest of the fisherman who says to the worm: "Come, let's go fishing."

The GDR's minister for *Länder* and regional questions, Herr Preiss, had issued an invitation to Güstrow for a discussion of the relative merits of Schwerin and Rostock. The moderator had set up four chairs for a panel discussion. The three chairmen of the district administrative authorities took their places at the podium: Herr Kalendrusch, Herr Dr. Diederich, and Herr Brick. At the outset, I raised my hand and noted that while these three were authorized to administer the districts, I – as the chairman of the Council of Counties and Cities in *Vorpommern* – I was the first freely elected representative of a region, the region of *Vorpommern*, and so our region was entitled to the fourth chair at the podium. I then took my seat at the podium, where I represented the interests of the citizens of *Vorpommern*.

In the competition to be capital, Schwerin received the majority of the votes. And so we have a capital that requires of us *Vorpommern* a three to four hour drive – each way; a capital that has represented *Mecklenburg* for centuries and never had to so much as note the existence of *Vorpommern*; a capital whose orientation is toward Lübeck and Hamburg, which is why so many of its representatives show us their backs sooner than their faces. A government, in the end, that consults mainly with Schleswig-Holstein, where *Vorpommern* is out of the picture. Problems associated with the Oder River, for example, are largely unknown there. In my judgment, this decision runs contrary to the interests of *Vorpommern*. It does, however, serve to make it all the clearer why we in *Vorpommern* need a counterweight to bring things into balance.

Such a counterweight did seem to appear: the old structure of districts was dissolved. On December 31, 1990, the district administration authorities ceased to exist. Rostock and Neubrandenburg no longer had their own administrative authority over *Vorpommern*. Now, everything was concentrated upon the government in Schwerin. The *Ministerpräsident*, or chief executive for the *Land*, was Dr. Alfred Gomolka from Greifswald. Eight ministers belonged to his cabinet, three of them from *Vorpommern*. So there was general confidence that the government would not lose sight of the interests of *Vorpommern*.

The first big excitement arose when decisions were to be made about constituting and installing the agencies of the *Land*. Not only was the autonomy of county and town administrations called into question, but it was equally disturbing that of the 39 agencies already planned, only three were to have their headquarters in *Vorpommern*. A second draft document, generated as a result of our protests, spoke of forty-six agencies, nine of them in *Vorpommern*. The area comprising *Vorpommern* has about one third of the population and one third of the territory in our new *Land*. In the end, we accomplished a more balanced distribution of agency headquarters. The efforts of *Vorpommern*'s representatives on behalf of Greifswald were crucial; the administrative appellate court and the administrative court as well as the fiscal court are now located in Greifswald, thus strengthening and supporting the continued existence of the faculty of law at the Ernst Moritz Arndt University. Our next priority was to locate and secure the necessary buildings for these courts.

Viewed from the perspective of *Vorpommern*, the nucleus of administration lies in planning at the *Land* level. Yet all planning still originated in Rostock, Neubrandenburg and Schwerin. Since *Vorpommern* was thus still regarded not as a single entity, but arranged along the old district lines instead, the Council of Counties and Cities of *Vorpommern* established a working group for regional planning and in 1991 had the planning firm Urban System Consult draw up a regional planning overview for *Vorpommern*. It took a lot of effort to persuade the counties and cities, again and again, to reach the necessary compromises in individual counties so as to be able to continue speaking with a single voice for the region, so that our essential points were articulated clearly. Since this work received no funding from the *Land*, and was paid for by the counties and communities, a number of communities had difficulty setting aside the necessary funding in a year that was forcing them to make drastic budget cuts. But in the end a planning overview for *Vorpommern* was produced in an interesting and appealing format. We were able to provide this overview to agencies, ministries and investors at all levels. Legislative representatives and planning authorities at the *Land* level, in the federal government, and throughout the European Economic Community were informed in this way as well. [Jürgen] Möllemann, then German minister of state for economic affairs, reported to us that this presentation had given him a good orientation regarding the issues facing our region. A copy was handed to the federal chancellor personally. This effort was especially helpful in dealing with the *Land*'s ministry for economic affairs. We pursued a dual objective there: on the one hand, we wanted *Vorpommern* to be its own region for planning purposes. At the same time, though, it was important to us that planning take place not only at the *Land* level, but also – and if possible, primarily – as a collaborative effort among the local authorities within the region.

Dr. Becker Marx was a great help in all these planning projects. He was a former *Landrat*, or county executive, and planning policymaker in Rheinland-Pfalz. He served as an advisor to Mayor Lastovka in Stralsund and lent important assistance to the Council of Counties and Cities on the regional planning overview – and with his arguments before the ministry of economic affairs. Thus we were able to attain both our goals: first, *Vorpommern* was adopted as a planning region and the Hanseatic cities of Stralsund and Greifswald named jointly as the new region's center; and second, a *Land* planning association, whose members are sent by local governments, has a voice in setting the planning agenda.

The *Land* planning agency was installed in Greifswald and took up its work on December 1, 1992. Unfortunately, there were difficulties at the start, because the staff of the other former district planning offices appealed the necessary termination of their old positions to the labor court, and so the planning slots for the *Vorpommern* area remained unfilled for months. To that extent, *Vorpommern* lags two and a half years behind the other planning regions in the *Land*, which will have serious consequences for all projects and their budgets.

The most important element for such planning is the transportation grid. The Prussians had known this. In 1836, they had built roads from Berlin to Stralsund. Later, the railroad routes were added, joined finally by the ferry between Sassnitz and Trelleborg, Sweden – the "Royal Line". Under Hitler, the *Autobahn* was built from Berlin to Stettin. Other than that, virtually nothing was undertaken to link the region to the larger transportation grid. The GDR did assign the region north of the Peene River administratively to Rostock. But during forty years of socialism, the rail line between Stralsund and Rostock remained a single track. Passenger trains would routinely stop mid-route and wait patiently until the train coming in the other direction had passed. The *Autobahn* from Berlin to Rostock did finally get built, and it now helps Rostock to attract passengers from the Scandanavian ferries. *Vorpommern* is practically uncoupled from the rest of Germany. For that reason, it is urgently important that an *Autobahn* be built to open up the region, that gaps in the railway system be filled in, and that the ports at Sassnitz-Mukran be expanded and better connnected to the transportation grid. From its first meeting on, the Council of Counties and Cities has been working toward the goal of building a highway or even an *Autobahn* from the Prenzlau section of Berlin to the two ports on the island of Rügen. In Neubrandenburg, the intention had been to construct an *Autobahn* from Lübeck to Stettin via Neubrandenburg. Then *Vorpommern* would have been simply out of luck. The economic axis through our region would have lain dormant for a long time. So we worked to summon all the persuasiveness and sense of urgency we possibly could for our presentations. We besieged the *Land* government and the legislature as well as the federal legislature and administrative offices. The federal minister of transportation's voice carried a lot of weight. Greifswald's Senator Vossberg went to the representation of *Mecklenburg-Vorpommern* in Bonn and made sure the minister of transportation was fully aware of our priorities. Now there is a draft federal plan for transport routes. An *Autobahn* from Lübeck to Prenzlau will be extended far enough to the north that it will reach the Stralsund-Greifswald area, thus making the east-west connection possible as well as the north-south line.

Plans also include connections to the ports on the island of Rügen. Contact was made quickly and often with the president of the *Reichsbahn*, the former East German rail system, clearly presenting and emphasizing the importance of our economic axis and of including the ports on Rügen. And recently, definite efforts in the same direction have become apparent from their side. The new president of the *Reichsbahn* office in Schwerin was surprised during his amicable first official visit to the Greifswald city hall. He told me with pride, and certain of great praise, that there was now a direct train route from Cologne to Binz. I told him that this was very nice, but it missed the area of our primary interest. Then I pointed out to him how the coordinates of Vorpommern lie. He was not the only one who later assured me that he had not only not forgotten this lesson about *Vorpommern*, but that he accepted this perspective as valid.

A further point of emphasis for transport and traffic in *Vorpommern* was driven primarily by the southern counties and concerns the restoration of the rail line between Berlin and Usedom. And finally there was some discussion about possible air connections to Ahlbeck and to what had been military airports at Schmoldow or Tutow.

Regarding the promotion of a zone along the Oder River, I had repeatedly contacted both the Lord Mayor of Berlin, Herr Diepgen, as well as the Minister-President of Brandenburg, Herr Stolpe, both verbally and in writing. In the winter of 1991-1992, I was sent a development concept that the city of Berlin and the *Land* Brandenburg had together commissioned for a promotion zone on both sides of the Oder. This study was submitted to the finance ministry in Schwerin at the same time. To my disappointment, I have never heard an active reaction to these plans, except that this plan had been merged with other initiatives for a (larger) Euro-Region.

At a conference in Cottbus for trans-border regions in 1991, I had the opportunity to meet Messrs. von Malchus and Gabbe. Both are extensively involved in working for the trans-border Euro-region along the Netherlands' border. Both of them showed great interest in *Vorpommern* and are always ready for intensive collaboration. Both joined me in planning a meeting that took place in Zinnowitz and Usedom in December, 1991. The meeting was also sponsored by the Council of Counties and Cities of *Vorpommern*, with an interested delegation from the *Województwo* of Szczecin and attentive observers from the Swedish and Danish sides situating the meaningful conversations that took place within the proper frame of reference. At that meeting, the Council of Counties and Cities established a working group for a trans-border European Region *Pomerania* on both sides of the Oder. *Landrat* Haedrich from Pasewalk assumed leadership, with the lively assistance of newly-arrived *Landrat* Waack from Ueckermünde, with his years-long experience on the Euro-Region along the French border. We were delighted that the German working branch for this region could be finally constituted and a declaration of corresponding intent on the part of the *Województwo* could be presented on November 8, 1992. Several eastern counties of the *Land* Brandenburg had joined the *Vorpommern* counties as well.

As chair of the Council of Counties and Cities, I had made contact quite early with the League of Communities in Southern Sweden and its chair, Philipp Moding. A whole series of encounters and joint events and a variety of helpful connections followed. Within two years, for example, six sister city relationships were established between Skåne, Sweden's southernmost province, and *Vorpommern*.

As far as the European Economic Community is concerned, it remains an open question to what extent one may see it as binding that on the map in Brussels *Vorpommern* is labeled as a region in the EEC area. By paying a visit to our counterparts at the EEC central offices in Brussels, my co-worker, Herr Klimpel, and I tried to get a comprehensive view of the issue and to press our case there.

An essential basis for all further activities promoting the existence of *Vorpommern* is whether, in the long run, the people of *Vorpommern* will be able to represent their identity with a unified voice. Three factors are significant here: first, the administrative unity of *Vorpommern* within the *Land* of *Mecklenburg-Vorpommern*; second, the constitutional backing for a higher league of communities – a regional league; and third, the practical shaping of region-level tasks and responsibilities.

The *Land* association as well as the Council of Counties and Cities had come out quite early in favor of a unified administration for *Vorpommern* as a partial *Land*. In the process of the arduous negotiations on county area reforms, the self interests of the various counties and *Land* councillors quickly came into confrontation to such an extent that a unified process and speaking with a single voice was not always possible. In fact, some representatives saw their particular salvation in the destruction of *Vorpommern*'s unity. This was actually welcomed by some members of the *Landtag* and of the *Land* government. This way, the whole *Vorpommern* cause would quickly be discredited and a divide-and-conquer approach would appear sensible on several points. In fact, in the re-drawing of county lines there is much disagreement on whether the new counties should stay with the traditional configuration along the *Land* boundary between the old *Mecklenburg* and the old Vorpommern, or whether counties should be created that are no longer defined by the riverbeds that had formed natural dividing lines since the ice age. This discussion has become dramatic in the area of Ribnitz-Damgarten, where, in addition to the interests of the individual localities, an extraordinarily powerful lobby is active in government and *Landtag*.

And yet, a majority seems to have emerged in support of including a clause, in the new *Land* constitution for *Mecklenburg-*

Vorpommern, that will allow the formation of a regional structure. After the county lines are re-drawn and the next local elections are held, it will be a matter of how the various areas of responsibility turn out, and to what extent the localities are prepared to work together, that decides whether a regional authority for *Vorpommern* – and possibly a corresponding one for *Mecklenburg* as well – will take shape. Then *Vorpommern* would be represented in one place, and in certain relevant matters no longer would two *Mecklenburg*er and one *Vorpommer* have to figure out together what is best for our region.

Many, many discussions – in the *Vorpommern* Council of Counties and Cities, among its members, in the working group for regional planning, and in the working group for the Europa-Region, with delegates to the *Land* legislature and with the aid of representatives in the *Bundestag*, discussions within the government and at the federal level in Bonn as well as at the *Land* level in Schwerin, but also in the beautiful *Löwenschen Saal* in the Stralsund city hall – have all advanced these initiatives for *Vorpommern*. One can only hope that in the foreseeable future such results will be achieved as equal opportunity for citizens of *Vorpommern* in the Federal Republic of Germany demands.

Das Land Mecklenburg-Vorpommern

The first democratic elections in the German Democratic Republic took place on March 18, 1990. In them, the *Volkskammer*, or general legislature, of the GDR was democratically elected for the first and last time. New ministers took up the new positions. Two of them came from Greifswald: Herr Terpe, Professor of Mathematics, took charge of the higher education system. Herr Benthin, Professor of Geography, became Minister for Tourism. That was profoundly useful for us in Greifswald at the round table and, later on, at city hall. For one thing, it meant we could raise our concerns very quickly and directly; for another, it gave us an important source of information. We were still living in the age of the message in a bottle. Even conversations on the telephone were extraordinarily difficult: not only were the relatively few phones and phone lines constantly overloaded; the people one needed to talk to were constantly changing as well. New people had new responsibilities, old institutions were being dissolved, new ones being created. Everyone who had any responsibility was constantly playing a high-stakes game of "who's who?". The new legislature and the new government did try to pass meaningful laws and statutes, and they did so effectively. But as early as July/August of 1990 it became clear that their main task would be the self-dissolution of the GDR. The more the central state authority with its institutions and ministries were dissolved, the more uncertain the status of law and administration became, and the more steadfastness was required of the one remaining stable administrative level, the local communities with their deputies and department heads. How often did we drive to Berlin to large gatherings of community officials, so that we could at least receive verbal explanations about developments and rulings, the written (and thus binding) version of which might not be made available to us for weeks – or not at all. When we brought up our concerns with Herr de Mazière, the head of the government, during a visit he made to Greifswald, he remarked to us that, while he understood us completely, his time was quickly coming to an end, while we would go on existing for a long time.

The constitution for localities originated in those months, although it was passed and made available to us only after most of the preparation period for a municipal charter had passed, leaving us without a foundation for dealing with some very basic issues. Also dating from his time was the law concerning municipal property, which demanded an enormous amount of work from us within a very short time.

As the central government was supposed to be dissolved, the old GDR system of districts had to cease its existence as well. For a rather long transition period, a special agent was named for each district. For the district of Rostock it was Herr Kalendrusch, for Schwerin Herr Dr. Diederich, and for Neubrandenburg it was Herr Brick. Their most important role had to do with the period October 3-14, 1990. In that time, and even a bit earlier, their signature was the sole authority within their respective areas, because the ministries of the GDR had disbanded before October 3, and after October 2, there was no longer a GDR. But there weren't any *Länder* yet, either. Viewed exactly, the GDR as a whole joined the Federal Republic as a new *Bundesland* and didn't separate into five new *Bundesländer* until two weeks later. For this brief period, the sole representatives of any administration within this new GDR-*Bundesland* were the district special agents, each for his or her own area.

On October 14, elections were held for the *Land* legislatures, and thus the representatives of the new *Länder.* In *Mecklenburg-Vorpommern*, the *Landtag* was constituted on October 25. From that day on, the *Land* was fully operational. Accordingly, the district authorities had to accomplish one of the newly created words of the day: by December 31 they had to "wind down" the administrative functions of the district. But we who worked at the community level had to move, during these months of 1990, by leaping from one stone to the next, so to speak, through the racing stream of the *Wende*, all the while maintaining and enhancing continuity.

Much later, when I was reporting in Osnabrück on this period of shifting structures, I was met with sheer envy on the part of West German local government officials: how gladly would they have spent even half a year governing without feeling the tug at the reins by the *Land.* Likewise, the transitions – from one state to another, from one currency to another, and from one set of laws to another – held many opportunities but also many dangers. We can only hope that we have used this time in ways that are sensible and responsible for the city and for our region.

Once the *Landtag* and the government had been elected, I was made to feel the results both immediately and, in the end, very bitterly. Our partner city, Osnabrück, had invited my wife and me to their annual festival. Full of new and positive impressions, I returned on October 26 to Greifswald from this, my first official visit in Osnabrück. The first bit of news I heard was that our senator for finance, Frau Kleedehn, had left Greifswald. Dr. Gomolka had named her minister of finance for the *Land*. They both were from the Greifswald neighborhood of Eldena. For better or for worse, I had to support Dr. Gomolka and wish him a good start.

This began a period of severe trials, both for the city administration and for me personally. Next the director of the finance office in Greifswald came to me on December 12 and told me he would be leaving the city administration on December 16. At the request of the minister of finance – his former supervisor in Greifswald's city hall – he would be taking over the construction and direction of a tax office for the *Land*. By the end of the year, it turned out that six additional members of the finance office left Greifswald's city government and joined the *Land* tax office's staff. All these resignations were subjected to legal review, but they could be neither blocked nor postponed, so that from the end of 1990 until March of 1991 the Hanseatic City of Greifswald was practically without a finance office. December brought in a number of allocations, some planned, some unexpected, with a total funding increase of 40% over the previous months. Suddenly, city administration had a substantially greater scope of action. Thus, on December 21, the senate faced the job of sorting out finances for wide-ranging measures by the end of the year – i.e. within four working days.

This turbulent time, extending through all of 1991, regularly drove the *Bürgerschaft*, the press, and parts of the population to their wits' end. For a long while, the rows of representatives and the headlines of the press were full of rumors about tens of millions in unexplained spending. In the final accounting for the year 1990, all that remained open was a sum of less than DM10,000 in excess salary payments during the month of the currency changeover, most of which could not be reclaimed from employees who had in the meantime moved from Greifswald to various *Länder* in the old

Federal Republic.

So it happened that the constituting of the *Land* gave the first impulse that led to a climate of mistrust toward the mayor, the senate, and eventually the *Bürgerschaft* assembly as well. Had it not been for the energetic and highly competent work of Herrn Lipsky, who left the finance ministry in Kiel to become our new senator, rebuilt the finance office, and put the city's finances back in order, the consequences of this turbulence would have been much more serious. In return he got many months of bitter conflict in the senate, because he had to reduce the unfulfillable demands of the various offices and departments to the scale of the means actually available. In 1991 he took office with a budget that had not been passed, the draft of which contained 44 million in unfunded expenditures. In June the budget was passed with a deficit of 20 million. In November it was updated with only a 10 million deficit, and at the year's end the required reserves of several million were in place within the framework of a now balanced budget.

This result, achieved through hard struggle, split the senate into a camp of adversaries who did their best to make life difficult for each other. Senate meetings resembled bitter combat. If it had been possible for us to maintain sensible bookkeeping throughout, much energy would have still been available to us that instead was consumed in this ongoing friction. In this way, the constituting of the *Land* exacted a harsh price from the Hanseatic City of Greifswald.

Still, the give and take between *Land* and city yielded a series of improvements as well. How often did Greifswald's senators visit the respective ministries [in Schwerin] in order to secure the appropriations or permits they needed to do their work? How much hard work did *Land* and city together put into mastering the ins and outs of the federal legal system? How much correspondence helped us to grasp – often contrary to our thinking and our intuition – how the laws dictate certain practices?

After a long period of controversies, of insights gained, of briefings and technical discussions, the workings of city administration have become more and more normalized. And yet a small number of decisions from the fall and winter months 1990/1991 leave questions open even today that result from the fact that, at that time, legal rulings by the *Land* did not yet exist, and legal rulings by the federal government were not sufficiently known or not adequately understood.

Insiders will know the stories regarding the *Martinstift* home, the polyclinics, the office of health in the workplace, swimming and diving sports center, county cultural center, and *Elboblock 36*. These and other issues had to be decided at a time in which the necessary legal standards did not exist. They weigh upon the efforts of our respective staff members like a never-ending tapeworm. Some of these cases will have to be resolved in court.

All the new *Länder* had difficulty at first finding a common designation. Former GDR, Five *Länder*, New *Länder*, Newfiveland, and the like were being used. All these *Länder* have to work their way out of a particularly difficult chapter. Created during the first legislative session out of structural chaos, they were supposed to begin redrawing county lines and to reach a sensible outcome, soon enough – if possible – for the waves caused by such a re-distribution of territory to dissipate somewhat before the next local elections.

One palpable date for us in Greifswald came when *Mecklenburg-Vorpommern*'s chief executive, Minister President Gomolka, was replaced by Minister President Seite and his altered cabinet. I can still picture clearly the afternoon when a group from Greifswald and *Vorpommern* sought out Dr. Gomolka in his offices during his last hours in office. But time moves on quickly, and all the turbulence has gradually given way ever more clearly to the normal routines of everyday work.

Yet one important question still causes agitation: What rights does local government have, and what rights fall to the *Land*? Legislators at both levels represent the same voters. To what extent can the principle of self-administration by local communities be upheld, and what point is the authority of the *Land* in force? A string of quarrels has resulted, either from legislators at the *Land* level being insufficiently informed and respectful of the work of local governments – perhaps not being sufficiently interested in that work – or, that the consultants from Schleswig-Holstein have in their heads a different model of the state than what one finds in the GDR's communal constitution. This gave rise to a number of debates, some of them quite lively, and some bias could probably be found on both sides.

We county executives and mayors in *Vorpommern* were quite proud of our association of communities, the Parliament of Counties and Cities. Especially in the first months, we represented not only the interests of the region, but also concerns at the level of local self-administration. As an aside, it also bears mentioning that we learned from the German League of Cities that our registered association, the *Vorpommern* Parliament of Counties and Cities, is unique in all of Germany insofar as here counties and cities have formed a single association and represent their interests jointly.

Scarcely had Dr. Gomolka been elected Minister President at the end of October, 1990, when I began besieging him with requests to schedule a hearing with the *Vorpommern* Parliament of Counties and Cities as well as with representatives of the counties and cities in *Mecklenburg*. The date was set for January 5, 1991. The president of the *Land* Parliament, Herr Prachtl, attended, as did the legislative caucus leaders, the members of the cabinet, several mayors and county officials, the chair and chief executive officer or our Parliament of Counties and Cities, and the freshly arrived director for *Mecklenburg-Vorpommern* of the *Land* Parliament of Rural Counties. There was an initial, thorough airing of positions on the question of how the interests of the voters could be represented, by the localities on the one hand, and by the *Land* on the other, according to the principle of subsidiarity – only what can not be satisfactorily addressed at the lower level becomes the responsibility of the higher level. One outcome of this meeting was a consensus that both the *Land* legislature and the ministries would remain open to mutual consultation with the localities and to scheduled hearings like today's had been. In the time that followed, this has occurred. Only, the minutes of the session referred not to the community leagues [*Kommunalverbände*] but instead to community leadership leagues [*kommunale Spitzenverbände*] – a term with which we were not familiar then, but which was to have major consequences for us. Part of the ensuing difficulties came from the Federation of Towns and Cities, which had reservations about allowing equal standing for our organization, composed as it was of both cities and counties; and the Parliament of Rural Counties opposed it outright. The other difficulties lay mainly with the Ministry of the Interior, which was responsible for local issues, and which regularly neglected us by inviting only the groups established in the west – centered in Schwerin and represented by their business offices there – and sometimes not even bothering to announce their events to us in *Vorpommern*, who had spent so much time and energy on this matter and on behalf of our region. With the benefit of hindsight, I have to admit that our association would have been overwhelmed with a multitude of responsibilities. Only, at that point we had not yet come to this realization, as we were the only representatives of localities organized at the *Land* level, and, for an initial period, we were in fact ahead of the curve in representing the interests of local entities.

In the meantime, the field of tension between the localities and the *Land* has been addressed and regularized by a network of laws, directives, statutes and local rulings, so what were initially large areas of mutually overlapping interests are now increasingly staked out and delimited into smaller "parcels".

One essential point remains open: a constitutional ruling and a possible practical role for higher leagues of localities – the regional leagues.

For the Hanseatic City of Greifswald, one area of serious interest is determined by the *Land*: the area of education and culture, which applies not only to school and theater, but above all affects the life of the university. Here direct determination by the *Land* is felt especially keenly, since our city sees itself as a center of culture and education for *Vorpommern.*

The Federal Government

For those of us who learned to be citizens of the GDR, there has always been a centralized state. Independence – in fact, the quality of these *Länder* being their own state to some extent – was something we grasped only slowly. The image that they present is still often confusing, multifaceted, and contradictory. Also, the *Länder* have a substantial degree of egoism, which drives their interests against each other and, often enough, is directed against claims from the regions of the former GDR. Since the *Länder* are are responsible for questions of culture, it is no wonder that in the five new *Länder,* and in cultural matters in particular, there are often especially large barriers to be overcome. The federal government, by contrast, has a program focused on German unity and the community of Europe. The greatest of hopes are attached to it; it is what Germans have on their TV screens every evening. It is the true advocate for the new *Länder.* It allocates most financial resources. Its laws are all about the federation, with adjustments made in accordance with the German unification treaty. It is the guarantor of stability in politics and in the currency. This is how we see it and what we expect of it. Our expectations were so high that, on the day of German unification, we saw only the fulfillment of our wishes, but not the extent of the difficulties that lay ahead. Now our vision has grown keener in the new *Länder,* and, gradually, in the realm of the old Federal Republic as well.

Our hopes are directed, nevertheless, primarily at Bonn. [translator's note: As this text was written, in 1993, the transition from Bonn to Berlin as the German capital had not yet been completed.] In Bonn, there is a permanent representative of the *Land Mecklenburg-Vorpommern,* a post held by Herr Vossberg for a while, who gave up his post as the senator for buildings and construction in Greifswald to accept it. Our members of the *Bundestag*, Herr Adam (*CDU*) – a former representative in our Greifswald *Bürgerschaft* – and Herr Kuessner (*SPD*) – a former member of the democratically elected people's assembly of the GDR – are in Bonn. The federal ministers Frau Merkel and Prof. Krause, both from *Mecklenburg-Vorpommern*, are also there. Advocates for our interests are there. And not least among them – often regarded with hostility and ridicule, and yet a rock of stability and an unshakeable partisan of German unity – Chancellor Helmut Kohl. He is the one we have to thank for a powerful sign of shared German purpose, second only to the reunification itself: the *Bundestag*'s decision to move the capital to Berlin. To be sure, the interests of many in the old Federal Republic are at work undermining this decision. But it falls under the verdict of the greatest god in German society – the Deutschmark. The once-divided city of Berlin has a long way to go before it emerges from the wild swings of the transition period. But once this change of capitals is realized, then we in *Vorpommern* with our north-south axis will be far better off than we are now with Bonn, which lies so far to the west.

For our region, the federal transport infrastructure plan is, of course, hugely important. Probably only a few people realize how much we owe to the efforts of Federal Transport Minister Krause and his understanding of the interests of our region. The route of the planned Autobahn A-20 seems now to be set in accordance with our interests. Yet the fate of the ports of Sassnitz and Mukran, with their need of a link to the mainland, remains all too uncertain. Essential decisions concerning the shutdown of Greifswald's atomic power plant and the disposal of its nuclear fuels continue to be made in Bonn. But above all, the question remains, whether the International Thermonuclear Experimental Reactor (ITER), a key research project for all countries on earth, will be located in Greifswald – a matter that Bonn must take part in deciding, and then promoting, both nationally and internationally. In Bonn – and in Brussels – it will also be decided in what way the region along the Oder River will receive a special subsidy similar to the present border zone subsidy (for communities along the border that, until recently, divided East and West Germany) or as a European Region.

In Bonn we had to put up an intense fight to preserve our Greifswald University – which has been in existence since 1456 and survived plague, war, inflation and two dictatorships, but which almost fell victim in the first year of German unity to budget cutbacks, because Germany is 'so poor' after all.

But in Bonn decisions have been made, the effects of which we can already clearly feel. My first and immediate trip to Bonn was about expanding the telephone network. I was able to urge that the contracts for the comprehensive expansion of telecommunications not be awarded exclusively to the telecom companies, as had been the case thus far, but that the large electronics companies had to be granted these contracts, so that the work be accomplished quickly. I was surely not the only one who lobbied along these lines, since the change also required a formal decision by the *Bundestag*. But very soon after that visit, a representative of the Siemens corporation came to me at city hall and reported that my efforts had played a significant role in Siemens' decision in favor of *Mecklenburg-Vorpommern*, and that they would set to work in Greifswald first. No one talks about it any more, but there are already several thousand new phone lines operating in Greifswald, and the trenches for buried cable already extend to the outskirts of our city. One visible landmark of these efforts is the new telecom tower on *Beimlerstraße*.

In the summer of 1990 a group of experts from the Federal Ministry of Finance under the leadership of Ministry Director Schill appeared in Greifswald. I was able to show them the city, and took them on a tour, especially in the area of *Wachsmann-, Bau-, Böhmke-, Burg-*, and *Wiesenstraße*. There we discussed the question of where the tax income from trades and small middle-class businesses would go in the coming years. These discussions evidently had a profound effect. On two separate occasions I was later sought out by members of this visiting group. Both times I was told that that first visit in Greifswald and my analysis had played a decisive role in the federal decision, in 1991, to disburse the so-called investment allowance directly to the local authorities in the new *Länder*, in order to promote new infrastructure as rapidly as possible. As a result, Greifswald was able to allocate more than 20.7 million marks for repair and maintenance of school buildings, old age and convalescent care homes, and social services.

So *Vorpommern* and Greifswald aren't always in a hopeless working situation; rather, I often had the impression that our region meets with more understanding in Bonn than, say, in Kiel, the capital of our partner *Land*, Schleswig-Holstein. And so I would say that the greatest support for our Hanseatic City of Greifswald during these difficult years came from our partner city, Osnabrück, and the federal government in Bonn.

A Look Back at Socialism

Justice has been a challenge for peoples and princes since the beginning of human time, the subject of holy scriptures in Judaism, Christianity, and Islam, a task that has occupied continents and cultures. Humankind's yearning for justice, and the effort to achieve it, is a driving force throughout history. Justice in society is the central social question. Shared justice in cities and communities is a primary aim for local government in waterways management, housing, fee and tax assessment, and many other areas.

When Karl Marx saw private ownership of the means and instruments of production as the root cause of injustice in modern society, he confronted medieval and bourgeois society with a demand for justice. Following his concept, powerful forces were mobilized for expropriation, for collective ownership of the means of production, for the erection of socialism and communism – a society of justice. Whole decades and continents stood under this Marxist concept.

Amid a global atomic arms race, the "free world" and the "socialist camp" faced off after the second World War. The one neglected justice, the other trod on freedom. The one called for "peace in freedom", and the other asserted "Socialism: that's freedom". Both were ready to sacrifice freedom, and both were preparing to wage global nuclear mass murder. But then socialism collapsed like a house of cards. From the Elbe to Vladivostok, the system of a world power crumbled. Why? Because writers, church powers, the intelligentsia with their *Solidarność* and candlelight vigils carried the day? Because mass flight across the wall and the iron curtain left functionaries at an impasse? Because the military might of the Western nations had driven socialism to its knees? The socialist functionaries knew better. Almost without fighting back at all, they gave up their own system.

Without many compunctions, they could have put down resistance in their countries. The army, police, state security apparatus and the omnipresent, fully trained and disciplined civil war troops – and in the GDR, the factory battle groups, whose numbers exceeded those of the people's army – could have made short work of rounding up the heads of oppositional groups into the already prepared concentration camps, and liquidating them. They didn't do it. Without resistance, the majority of the leading functionaries allowed the collapse of their system to go forward. They knew that there was nothing left to hold on to. Their economy was at its end, their money was worthless, their reserves were spent. They gave up their system. Their system was bankrupt and had failed. Why?

Three causes stand out.

They had abolished private ownership of the means of production, and with it the struggle for survival in competition, and the give and take of a free market. Instead of the free market, they invented the regulating mechanism of a planned economy. But it proved impossible to control matters and actually fulfill these plans. Five year plans subjected the economy to a regime of the sort Bertolt

Brecht sang about:

Ja macht nur einen Plan	Sure, make yourself a plan,
Seid nur ein großes Licht	And be a shining light
und macht noch einen zweiten Plan	Go on and make a second plan
gehn tun sie beide nicht.	Neither one will work.

And yet the plans were made to work. The needs of the people and of the market were overridden and subjected to those priorities that Marxist/Leninist party philosophy dictated.

The place of the free market was taken by the planned economy, and this was subordinated to ideology. In the West, whoever succeeds in the free market has a share of power. In the East, whoever put himself at the disposal of the ideology had a share of power under socialism. Here lay the center of power under socialism. The political slogans on the many red banners were the threadbare equivalent of the thousandfold brightly colored product offerings in the free economies. From the center of power, the ideologues here and the producers there tried to win over their mass society and their consumers. Here, as there, it was all about power.

The power in the East was held by the ideologues, since they regulated the planned economy. These people who called themselves materialists put their idealism into people's heads in the form of their ideology. Everyone owed this ideology their conviction, obedience, or at least constant kowtowing. The more unequivocally one submitted to the ideology, the closer one was to the center of power. Whoever wanted to survive in socialism had to at least conform to the ideology, that was the minimum prerequisite. The mechanism of conformity was offered in many forms and across a broad range, from kindergarten to veteran's club.

Two counterforces stood in opposition to the ideology. These were, first of all, one's own interests. Where these could not be made to conform, they were repressed. The party provided for conformity, the state took care of the repression. The stealthy play of personal interests against people's publicly declared loyalty led to constant corruption on all levels and undermined the entire system. In order to keep at least the leading ideologues and functionaries in line, there were privileges tied to party membership. These in turn were felt, amid the generally prevailing scarcity of goods and services, to be unfair. The system identified itself with socialism, communism and justice. Injustice, in the form of privileges and corruption, called the whole system into question and left it with no credibility. However, the ideology was dependent upon credibility. Where that was lacking, repression and terror were necessary.

The other counterforce opposing ideology was constantly rising up in the name of science, research, and education. Even the slightest questioning by pupils in elementary school had to be met with efforts at persuasion and conformity – and thus silenced. The Ministry of People's Education, under Margot Honnecker, ruined whole generations of teachers and students with the schizophrenic balancing act of a science education under compulsory conformity with ideology. It was no coincidence that a riddle circulated: What's the relationship between God (*Gott*) and Margot? (The final *t* in Margot not being silent, the two words rhyme.) The answer: *Gott* is to Margot as education is to People's Education.

At the universities, the departments for Marxism-Leninism led the effort to prove the congruence of ideology and science. A whole string of arguments were used. In the process, they made clear to what extent professors, teachers, and other educators could be bought. And yet, science and truth could not be silenced. A constant effort worthy of Sisyphus was put forth, trying to roll the stone of ideology up the mountain of truth; it was a struggle in the face of logic and thinking and doubt and news reports, a struggle in equal measure against academic propriety and against Western television.

And so ideology and the functionaries of the system were subject to ongoing stress, fighting an uphill battle against the people's best interests and against their right to the truth. They could not win this struggle.

Once the economy could no longer be relied upon to meet even the most elementary needs of the population, the functionaries decided, evidently on their own, to stop using force to prop up an untenable system. The towering figure in this change of direction, with his call for *Perestroika* and *Glasnost*, was, of all people, the head of the party and state apparatus in the socialist camp, the highest-ranking comrade, Mikhail Gorbachev.

If the ideologically-steered, planned economy were continuing to meet the most essential needs of the people and of the state, then the functionaries would probably have cold-bloodedly taken their chances with an – already prepared – mass murder by means of gulag camps or civil war or military holocaust. Experience has shown that the broad mass of the population would have tolerated it. The weapons of mass destruction, the armies for waging civil war, and the gulag archipelago had been available for some time – well-prepared, trained and ready. No, the economy collapsed. That's what it was.

That's how socialism and communism failed. The capitalist economy, the social market economy, the free world proved in the war of economic camps to be the stronger. They won the cold war in a cold way. Socialism and communism failed. But the challenge to achieve justice remains.

Integration into the Free World

"Liberté, egalité, fraternité" was the rallying cry of the French Revolution. What has remained is liberty – freedom – as a key concept for Western bourgeois society. Freedom, and the individual's right to self-determination concerning one's self and one's property, is the central idea behind the dynamism that drives the developed, industrial states forward. That's why the phrase justifying the existence of the Western military alliance was: peace in freedom. That's why propaganda instructs us that we now live in the Free World.

And, in fact, we do now have, finally, the right to travel, for example. With their old GDR identity papers in their pockets, my four student-age children had been nearly everywhere within the first year – from Tiflis to Lisbon, from Egypt to Norway. There was hardly a single country in Europe that they left out. Now there is freely convertible currency. Now the German mark is so valuable that one is almost ashamed at how cheaply one can travel in the countries of the former Soviet block.

We were most excited about the freedom to express our opinions openly. But lo and behold, where it really matters, the fear of losing one's job is a more effective muzzle than it was in socialist times. But where it doesn't cost anything – or might even bring in some money – freedom of speech yields a lot of nonbinding blossoms. Swamp blossoms, too, sprout and reach up forcefully, with their "foreigners go home" and other irresponsible slogans.

After the socialist monopoly on press and media, after the era of the party daily *Neues Deutschland* and its offshoots, after the television programs *Aktuelle Kamera* and *Schwarzer Kanal*, we had the highest expectations of the free press. Now, truth would finally take its rightful place. But truth, as we discovered soon enough, is also a commodity. Just as the textile industry cuts and stitches fabrics to make clothes to put in stores, the truth is also nothing more than raw material for journalism tailored to a particular audience. What the people want to hear or see or read is what gets broadcast or printed – whether it be invention, lies, half-truths, or if need be, actually the truth. The main thing is: it sells. But, just as sharks eat all the little fish, the newspapers of our region disappeared from the market. Of course, they were all independent at first. Different papers represented different political parties and perspectives: *Die Norddeutschen Neuesten Nachrichten* (NDPD), *Die Norddeutsche Zeitung* (LDPD), *Der Demokrat* (*CDU*). But after a short time, they all gave up the ghost – there was just no commercial basis for them.

All the greater, therefore, was our hope for *Das Greifswalder Tageblatt*, a newly-founded mid-sized daily that began appearing on

September 29, 1990, shortly before the official unification. With generous good will, we put up with its early difficulties, its typos and hurried editions. With concern we noted that its reporters – most of them imports from the West – foregrounded their clichés and their political/social preferences. We accepted that they had no space to print corrections. We learned that even official press releases were paraphrased like hearsay and subject to being re-cast in the reporters' own words. I myself had to put up with being berated as a scoundrel and a thug, and became the object of their boycott. And there were regrettable mistakes. When all the mayors and city council presidents of our partner cities met in Greifswald, there was no mention of it in the paper. The day after the groundbreaking ceremony for our largest investment project, a ninety-million-mark wastewater treatment plant, the paper's title photo, instead, was of the reed organ that the *Christusgemeinde* church had received. In spite of all this, I had high hopes for this paper, because it was to be a daily for *Vorpommern*, and it would serve as a counterweight to the old, familiar *SED* press. But the *Greifswalder Tageblatt*, too, proved unable to stay afloat. It folded on February 12, 1993. Now the only daily paper that covers the old GDR district is the former *SED* party organ in Rostock, with some of the same editors as before. This *Ostseezeitung* has a monopoly. Without any regional competition, we are entirely in their hands – which will have clear consequences in the election year of 1994. A free press: for us, that means an independent monopoly [of former *SED* members, now re-named] *PDS* [Party of Democratic Socialism], carried by the brand of [tabloid publisher] Springer Inc. Of course there are still the *Bildzeitung* and other papers with a less regional focus. Still, the everyday face of the free expression of opinions is one of the most profound disappointments of the *Wende*.

There is freedom for almost anything that can be paid for. If the municipal administration is in dire and difficult financial straits, then there is no free self-administration, then all expenditures are tied to legally prescribed obligations, and then the *Land*'s community supervision office actually holds the reins that the mayor and

Bürgerschaft think they have in their hands. And so freedom is dependent upon ownership and property.

To the extent that this is true, one of the most important and immutable prerequisites for a free market economy is that land and real properties that had been collectivized be returned to their rightful owners. With its tendency to disrepair and dilapidation, socialism has shown that under collective ownership, no one had final responsibility for anything. Thus, clarifying and establishing ownership of property is at the heart of the transition from socialism to the free world. In Greifswald, we succeeded in having municipal real estate declared property of the city as of October 2, 1990, under GDR statutes. As far as I know, no other city in the former GDR managed to do that. Now, though, it is our job to return the houses and properties to their rightful former owners.

Starting back in November 1990 – months before we were required to do so – a group of attorneys and administrative specialists has been working to settle unresolved ownership questions. More than 2,000 claims have been submitted. With all their intensive efforts – all the while contending with a frequently improved, i.e. altered, legal situation – as of December 1992, they have succeeded in returning about 300 pieces of property to their owners. In other words, 300 out of 2,000 claims settled in two years of work, and waiting times of up to 12 years. Where ownership has not yet been established, nothing final can be done. City administration can only carry out the most urgent repairs. The tenants might contribute on their own, but their position remains quite uncertain, as their landlords are not yet in possession of the deed papers. In plain words: for about 1,700 pieces of property, the process of gradual decline continues. There are also owners who definitely want their property returned to them, but they have no idea what should become of it and are by no means ready to invest money in it. The banks, too, want to minimize their risk; they ask for guarantees. But without actual ownership, in cash or in real property, not much can be done.

City administration, too, has to adapt the way it works to these circumstances. All community credits require approval from the *Land*'s supervisory agency. And these, in turn, are guided by the municipal budget statements. Privately managed enterprises move more readily. In order to get things moving, the Hanseatic City of Greifswald moved parts of what it owns into enterprises, which can then operate more independently. 10,000 apartments were transferred to the limited partnership [GmbH] Apartment Construction and Administration Corporation, and 4,000 more to another limited partnership: the Greifswald Apartment and Shelter Corporation. The port, public transportation, energy supply, water and wastewater issues – all these will fall under the purview of the city works and its subsidiaries. The theater and computing center are so-called independent operations. Again and again, the mayor finds himself representing the city and its property as a stakeholder in such companies, where the *Bürgerschaft* has released these properties from its control while still requiring accountability from them.

It became clear to me for the first time just what that means, when, as mayor, I suddenly found myself presiding over the administrative board of the local savings and loan. Feeling a bit like a child on his very first day of school, I arrived in Berlin for a day and a half of instruction designed to teach all mayors and county administrators from the territory of the former GDR how we would have to go about guaranteeing and assuming responsibility for the savings paid into S&Ls by the citizens of our regions – and how the simple deposit and withdrawal offices from GDR days should now be developed and structured as full-service banks offering a wide range of services. That was in early September, 1990. By November 1, right on schedule, we had accomplished what we had been charged to do: a new governing board was elected for Greifswald's municipal and county savings and loan.

In the many meetings of the savings and loan's board, it became clear within what set of rules property can be dealt with creatively and responsibly. However, what is true of the savings and loan is true elsewhere as well. The degree of freedom is determined by our dealings with property and ownership. Here lies the actual basis of the dynamics of egoism. Socialism defied the logic of self interest, individual drive, and productive private property – and it failed. The new (for us) Western society of freedom derives its power from the unjust distribution of property and from the resulting tensions in the marketplace.

With great effort a network of laws has grown up over decades and decades that preserves this unjust freedom and its dynamic power, and yet strives to achieve a necessary measure of justice. The present result in the Federal Republic of Germany is called *soziale Marktwirtschaft* (social market economy). Many complicated regulatory systems of rights and obligations, of laws and discretionary provisions are now in effect and binding upon us, whether we are familiar with them or not. We focus on achieving justice. But in reality we operate under the written provisions of the so-called rule of law.

For many decades, many people, governments and nations have sought a third way, a formula for a society – both just and based on the rule of law – with the positive atttibutes both of socialism and of a free market economy. Almost all former citizens of the GDR want to have both freedom and the advantages of socialism. The benefits that bankrupted socialism should nevertheless be guaranteed for all. But there is no third way. Now there is only the "free world". The compromise that is possible is *soziale Marktwirtschaft*. Hopes for justice rest with concessions of a social nature, but peace within a society – and, in the end, among nations as well – depends upon justice. Constantly achieving this balance anew under the dominance of property and without the pressure of a socialist camp, and perhaps with unemployment that is both growing and irreversible, requires the most intensive of efforts. At the moment, in our region the loss of about 40% of the jobs must be counteracted by means of services for the early retired, for workers on short hours, for the unemployed, for recipients of social services, for those receiving training in new fields, for those employed on make-work projects and for others, not least of whom are the daily growing number of economic refugees coming from other countries.

As of 1990, the challenge of a socialist camp is no more. The challenges that justice presents to a free society based on property ownership must now be met by that society's own decisions. Job creation measures, housing assistance offices, homeless shelters, refugee housing, social services, and youth services continue to require the greatest exertions from city administrations, in Greifswald and elsewhere.

Another Sort of Adjustment

Of course this period of adjustments is shaped by many fundamental factors. But even in their midst, almost every case is an exception. In this extra chapter I would like to report on a special case that was of interest for the Hanseatic City of Greifswald. It is the influence of the military. For Greifswald, that influence was actually quite modest. The surrender of the city by the town major, Colonel Petershagen, to the Red Army on 29-30 April 1945, saved the city from destruction on the one hand, and on the other hand, saved it from becoming a Russian garrison. The National People's Army (NVA) of the GDR, too, had actually installed only its district headquarters in Greifswald. There were only a few troops and military personnel in Greifswald. But in the years before World War II, the state had acquired land for the *Wehrmacht* and built an air force hospital on it. This land continued to be used as a hospital after the war; then it was given to the university and its newly-founded workers' and farmers' institute for students working toward qualification for university entrance. In the novel *Die Aula* (The Auditorium) by Herrmann Kant, one can read more about this school.

But in 1955 the medical school of the university was converted entirely, then later only partially, into a department of military medicine, still part of the university but under the authority of the defense minister. This transformation caused quite a stir among the students and professors. There were disturbances. In the days before Easter, 1955, the city of Greifswald was surrounded by armored vehicles and cordoned off. 265 students were taken out of the auditorium and into temporary custody – several of them for months, and even years. One of them, Dr. Rintelen, now a district administrator, was held in prison for ten years. Every citizen of Greifswald was able to see the conclusion of these events from a distance. The steeple of the *Jakobikirche* was set on fire. Whether this was a diversionary tactic, sort of a smaller version of the *Reichstag* fire, could never be proven. But the fact remained that most of the medical students had to leave Greifswald. In their place officer candidates from the NVA arrived with their corresponding pay grades, filling lecture halls as university students as well. Enjoying great privileges not available to regular students, they had not only a substantial income, but they also had direct access to many career opportunities. With their help, the extensively middle-class and independent medical community was overrun with socialist outsiders. From the minister of health to the clinic directors, the leading positions in medicine were taken by these cadres loyal to the party and the state. The Military Medicine Section in Greifswald was the party's forge for new cadres to take control of the health care system in the GDR. Whoever studied here was assured a fine future. What was studied here was certainly medicine, but medicine for the healthiest members of society in their best years: for soldiers. This was a medical practice for emergencies, where the fundamentals of medicine are stood on their head – where the weakest are not cared for first; rather, among all the wounded, mainly those are worth treating who, if need be, can be sent back into battle – a medical practice that, in an emergency, does not serve the civilian population most severely impacted by the war, remaining far removed from the needs of the people who are neither armed nor protected.

Since the professors of the Military Medicine Section were

expected to play their role at the university while also answering to the ministry of defense, their role at the university was that of a trojan horse. The shift to military medicine inflicted harm on the University of Greifswald, even though, contrary to original plans, there continued to be a substantial number of civilian medical students in Greifswald.

In the period of the *Wende*, the arsenal of the Military Medicine Section naturally played an interesting role for the entire region. According to the colonels' testimony, however, it remained locked. Armed action against the people, whether planned or not, did not occur. In fact, there was general surprise when, in the spring of 1990, the newspaper carried a large photo of the entrance to this military base with the caption "Swords into Plowshares" . Would Greifswald now bring to fruition a phrase for which schoolchildren had just recently been most sternly punished? Was it true that military cadres of the *SED*, of all people, now embraced this goal? Were expressions from the Bible now finding such favor? What had happened?

An order of the day had been issued by Defense Minister Keßler, *SED* party member in the Modrow government, according to which military properties were released for private use, primarily by NVA officers, if such private use created jobs for their subordinate personnel. The colonels in the Military Medicine Section didn't need to be told twice. They promptly had a sixty-six-year lease in their pockets for the entire MMS grounds and all buildings on them, not quite free of charge, but pretty close. Straight away they founded a limited liability company; they were quickly joined by several university professors who, in entering Federal German public service at the university, would have been unlikely to pass scrutiny in regard to their socialist past in the GDR. [Note: Professors at the universities of the former GDR had to undergo a two-fold examination: first, of their political career and degree of involvement with the *SED*, and second, of their professional qualifications. Only then were they allowed to compete against outside candidates for the positions they had once held.]

As figurehead and money broker they found, of all people, the former head of outreach ministry for the Lutheran Church of (West) Germany. In this way, they presented themselves as the vanguard of *soziale Marktwirtschaft*. Here was a classic example of an insider deal: the old leaders of Honecker's state and a representative of the Deutschmark. Swords to plowshares. Is there something wrong with this motto? In November 1990, they presented a draft proposal for the creation of a non-profit organisation with supervisory board and financing plans, which on the one hand turned out to be part wish list and part poker card, and on the other hand was approved in an amended form. And so this annexation via order of the day encouraging ventures in the public interest still stands. Neither the university nor the city has succeeded in undoing it, because the minister for disarmament in the de Maziere cabinet, Herr Eppelmann (*CDU*), also approved the sisty-six-year lease, naturally without consulting anyone in Greifswald about it. Under similar circumstances, several leading figures in the NVA were able to purchase real estate and housing units at ridiculously low prices that no municipality, and certainly not Greifswald, would ever have made possible. "*Medigreif GmbH*" is the name of this showpiece of *Wende*-era maneuvering, and the corporation is already expanding (with what funds?) to a point that it now plays a role in determining the economic vitality of the region. Does it need mentioning, by the way, that the colonels, before relinquishing all but their academic ranks, and during their transformation into partners in the limited liability corporation, secured from the federal defense minister their official recognition as officers of the *Bundeswehr*?

To be sure, my view of this matter is not impartial. But how could it be different, knowing all of these things, when I see at the same time what struggles and strains normal and in many ways disadvantaged tradesmen and business people must go through as they adjust to the new structures? In any case, this extra chapter, and the realization of what it means for the situation in Greifswald, should be included.

"Wir sind ein Volk" (We are One People) – *Ossis* and *Wessis*

"Ein Volk, ein Reich, ein Führer", was what I heard as a child. The *Führer*, or leader, led us into catastrophe. The *Reich*, or empire, was dissolved. The Germans to the east of the Oder and Neisse rivers were driven out, and the rest of Germany was divided into zones of occupation. Three zones in the West retained their economic structure and united to become the Federal Republic of Germany. The Soviet-occupied zone had to join the experiment in socialist economy, endured the greater burden by far of the lost eastern lands and of reparations – and became the German Democratic Republic. The *Volk*, or people, supposedly remained one. This, at least, was the commonly held view: *"Wir sind ein Volk"*.

At its core, that sentence is entirely accurate. If the Germans in the West had found themselves under Soviet direction, they too would have developed into party opportunists, *Stasi* informers, fugitives from the republic, swarming into new housing in the cities, all the while dreaming of a little cottage in the woods. They, too, would have lived practically rent-free in dilapidated buildings and compensated for minimal pay with a maximum of public subsidies. They would have learned Russian and kowtowed and conformed. Had the Germans in the East ended up under the occupation of the Western allies, they would have already passed through their food phase, their clothing phase, their travel and building phases. They would have a respectable savings account balance in a hard currency and would consider changes in pay scales, annuities, taxes, and fees to be the most important news items. So who is better, *Ossis* in the east or *Wessis* in the west? At the core, we Germans are one people. But not on the surface.

You can see that walking down the street. You can spot Westerners by their overcoats, their suits, their briefcases, and the way they walk. What stands out is their self-confidence. A *Wessi* shows up like his products do: exquisitely packaged and bearing a label that says "I'm exactly the specialist you need." From an early age, he has learned to sell himself. Marketing, that's what we in the East didn't need, didn't learn, don't know how to do. We were the children of the planned economy, we were planned for, and all we had to do was make sure the planners put us in the right slot. Now we are exposed to the market economy. What we had learned was to produce, to distribute, to live with one another and to attend to one another. To assert ourselves in the marketplace – that's something only a few untrained, natural talents manage to do. The one thing we had to do was adapt. The hope of the *Wende* was: no more adapting. Its result: adapting squared. Adapting ourselves to the market economy, adapting ourselves to West German laws, adapting ourselves to to Federal German administrative principles.

And so the *Wessis* are our instructors, our paymasters, our bosses.

Learning itself is the simplest and most pleasant part. One can master it; it takes a while, it's interesting, and success does come. It is associated with travel and exchanges, and it alters our position by making it more solid. How many courses, exchange weeks, officials on loan, and consultants have fulfilled their obligations between Osnabrück and Greifswald? However, not everyone recognized and saw how great the additional burden was, what sacrifices of free time and family life are associated with it, and how, in administration, the routine succession of business days was missed, days that were needed for further learning and practice. Learning means lots of extra stress: at the same time, work needs to go on as usual. But the allocation of roles is as follows: *Ossis* learn, *Wessis* teach. And this also applies in a much more profound sense, because we *Ossis* have to learn to fit into a new system, and we'll always be comparing it with the old system. The *Wessis* have no need to do that. Their system has remained as it was; there's nothing new to learn. The loser has to learn; a victor doesn't need to.

A lot of fanfare accompanies the handing out of money. What a festive clanging of bells there was [in 1983] when Honecker got

[Bavarian Minister President Franz-Josef] Strauss to arrange a credit for the GDR of a billion marks. *Neues Deutschland*, the *SED*'s daily newspaper, hoped that the GDR was thus rescued once and for all. Now we know better. More than a hundred billion is flowing from the West to the East: many billions come as corporate investments, many more billions from the pockets of taxpayers arrive as subsidies for daily needs and to help with reconstruction, and there are also many billions in smaller parcels and in the housing market. For who is going to put the crumbling houses, neighborhoods and apartment buildings back in order? Most property owners in the East don't have the money. The rent doesn't cover expenses, and the municipalities have a mountain of prior credits to pay off. If a piece of real estate in the East is returned to a Westerner, he or she can hopefully put it back in good order. If it belongs to a former citizen of the GDR, he or she usually can not afford thorough renovations – no matter how urgently they are needed – and burden themselves with debt or sell the property and thus leave it up to Western money to put the house in good shape again. *Ossi* and *Wessi*: to a great extent, it's a matter of giving money and taking it. What we *Ossis* take, though, we must pay for with the loss of our past, with the collapse of the world that had been ours.

There are also certain areas of life where we *Ossis* can't learn fast enough; if we didn't, then essential things, things that we need for rebuilding, would have been lost. This is why directors of banks and savings and loans, jurists and attorneys, corporate leaders, marketing specialists and qualified administrators all come to us. In Greifswald there is a string of banks, most of them new, all led by directors from the West. There's a law faculty again at the university, and four courts in the city, all largely occupied by people who have moved here from the West. Large companies want to avoid risking a loss of market share, so they need marketing managers. The new business managers of city utilities, of Siemens AG, of the nuclear power plant – they are all Westerners. What else would they be? They are the new bosses.

Here in city hall, I have got to know three *Wessis* particularly well.

For the post of deputy mayor, whose portfolio includes the central office, the personnel office, the legal office, and other positions as well, the *SPD* was not able to find anyone from our own city. So an expert – as they are called – was brought in from the West. He had previously been his party's business manager in Hamburg. He would surely know what was what, we could surely put our trust in him. He quickly closed himself off and sought out allies within city hall. In no time at all, there was polarization among the department managers. Six months later, without the knowledge of *Bürgerschaft*, finance board, senate, and also without my knowledge, he had set up a line of credit for 50 million marks. Fortunately for us, he had it underwritten by a company that didn't exist. Surely he was well intentioned, but he did have a bit of the con man about him. After a bit more than a year, when he was no longer able to stay, he left behind a legacy of sharp conflict between the parties, as well as a number of jobs left undone.

His successor was an expert who felt called to politics. On the one hand he denied this description, but on the other hand, he divided the city hall into friends and enemies, approving all that the former did and publicly discrediting everything done by the latter. Often, he was sure how things stood even before he got the facts of a matter. Since I, as his superior, was not one of his friends, I experienced one of his abilities in an intense way: mobbing. He helped move things forward in several important ways in multiple areas, but he had also left behind lots of broken glass. It is difficult to say whether he helped us more or harmed us more. His most important assignment – to significantly reduce the number of staff positions and thus make possible a defensible budget plan for 1992 – he put off for months. Instead, he cut the capable finance senator (*CDU*), and only in the middle of August, two weeks before the senator from his own party was to take over the finances, did he announce a staffing plan that cut out 345 positions. In city administration and in the *Bürgerschaft*, he helped quarreling between the parties to reach unimagined heights – before leaving Greifswald again after ten months.

The new finance senator (*CDU*) was as young as he was capable. He took a thoroughly miserable situation, both in numbers and in pairing the right people with the remaining positions, and within only a few weeks he achieved stability. The budget, which had been drawn up with a substantial deficit, he managed to bring into balance over the course of the year. Entirely scrupulous and well versed in the law, he set off the sharpest conflicts within the senate and then stood his ground, since he had to cut many budget lines and maintain strict financial discipline. In broader administrative matters as well, he contributed substantially to our understanding of how to apply certain laws. He left because the deputy mayor had cut him out of the staffing plan and had been hard on him otherwise as well, and because I, as mayor, did not have the authority to keep him. He subjected everyone, including me, to his merciless criticism. He was humble and willing to work. But his very sensitive pride was unable to get over some of the humiliations imposed by our living conditions and some of the improper behavior born of our inexperience.

Other consultants and helpers brought us very unequal degrees of assistance, and we got to know them as people – people like we are, or at least like we could be. In one point, though, they were clearly different from us Easterners: they brooked no second guessing of their expert opinion, and they could rule the circle of their subordinates quite ruthlessly – and with a sense of entitlement. For one important position in our city I was able to hire someone from the West. We managed to move much together, spoke together often and got along well. Yet there was one thing that I could scarcely believe: that after more than two years, he still had his wife and children living in the West and had not moved them here, no matter how well he and they got along. The problem was the house. Building takes a long time, and one of the best-situated houses in the city was not good enough for him. "You should see my house, then you would understand. I owe it to my family to protect our property status." "Well," I said to him, "you see how I live and manage, and after all, I am the mayor here." "Yes," he said: "that's what you're used to." What else could I say? That one phrase, though, may be the single greatest barrier between *Wessis* and *Ossis*: "protecting our property status". Often enough, it occupies the place that our hopes had reserved for "solidarity".

From my Point of View

Now I have presented a number of my experiences and impressions from the *Wende* period, between 1989 and the spring of 1993 from my perspective and against the backdrop of my thoughts. Naturally my perspective is shaped by the facts that I am a Protestant pastor, was mayor for a while and have gotten to know the city, the region, and its inhabitants from this point of view. As a pastor, I have always been concerned with the situation in which people find themselves, how they respond to that situation, where they find strength, meaning, and daily purpose – and how they bring those things to bear in their lives. And so for me it is profoundly moving to register how, between the despair before the *Wende* and the despair after it, there was a time of great joy and hope that caught people up and carried them – how endurance, patience, hard work and hopeful confidence have been and still are at work in the daily lives of those who stayed, returned, or came here for the first time. The many who left are not part of the picture I have tried to describe.

As mayor I had to turn my attention away from individual decisions and fates, and focus on the overall context and the massive structural changes. I had to acquaint myself with an enormous number of specialized areas of knowledge, and find the framework that would leave the city and the region with the best possible prospects for the future.

While as a pastor I had been able to address myself primarily to the goodness and reliability of people, with a motto of "dare to trust", as mayor I was constantly dealing with people whose excesses, dissatisfaction, intolerance and egotism, whether personal or institutional, caused friction, stress and unreason.

I was prepared for reasonable discussion of pros and cons, compromise, agreement and action. That had carried me, in the days when everyone wanted to be "the people" or "one people" , to the leadership of the city. I was unprepared for naked partisanship that gets hung up on contradictions, uses rational and irrational arguments, does not shy away from back doors and detours, but is equally capable of charging like a bull straight through the china shop, or of implacably marching in place until its opponent is simply exhausted. But, more and more, that became the practice, as the *people* once again became the *populace*. While I used to preach that a belief, a conviction, is worthless if one is not ready to pay the price for it, now I was becoming acquainted with human behavior on the level of prices and costs, where – though in a different way than in the era of the *Stasi* – here, too, the friendly image of convictions is often enough less than a thin veneer.

As I placed my trust in understanding and reason, I was looking for compromise from the start. But when I headed for compromise, I had already lost in the eyes of those for whom reason and compromise are of no concern and who cared only about their own position, their advantage. But that is evidently everyday reality in political life, and it is certainly one of the reasons why, as I was voted in, thirty-one months later I was voted out. Of course I had, for my part, taken positions, especially with regard to *Vorpommern*, that gained me both friends and enemies, so that my persistence was not always welcomed. Certainly, there was a host of intrigues, a high degree of partisanship, and a number of ill-matched structural choices in the city charter, all of which eroded the ground on which I stood. Naturally, the press was actively involved in its own way. In the end I, too, dug in my heels, when the lack of objectivity and the unfairness were just too much for me. It was clear from the outset that I am no expert administrator. Nevertheless, the common denominator of the criticism leveled at me was administration. And so I am content that, in the end, a moderate deputy mayor and a steady, experienced successor in the mayor's post – both of them from the West – have been found, so that perhaps now the turbulence of my time in office can quiet down.

I have come to the conclusion that I have won, even though I had to relinquish my post. Almost all my positions on behalf of *Vorpommern* have come about, and the regional concept continues to have energetic advocates. In the city, meanwhile, the two main points of conflict were decided in ways I had fought for. First, the new budget plan for 1993 was passed on time and without deficits, thanks to the efforts of the two finance senators in succession charged with drawing it up. In fact, the minister of finance called it a model budget. Second, procedures at city hall have been brought more squarely in line with the new legal situation, and the wishful thinking of the *Wende* period is no longer assumed to be legitimate just because it was so democratic. For democracy is not just whatever people think and wish; it's what the majority has determined. And in Germany democracy is not immediate: it adheres to the laws created in the postwar decades and the elected representatives.

What exacted the most from me? One thing was the stress brought about by less than transparent conflicting interests and by carefully maintained points of friction. But the other is a profound shift in my estimation of the *Wende* period. In 1949, at age sixteen, I was certain that that it would take at least 35 years before the occupying powers would leave and the unity of the fatherland could be regained. Now it has in fact taken 40 years. For me, this entire time was like a single arc of tension. When this tension was released with the fall of the wall on November 9, 1989, it was like a dam giving way. Even today, I have to be mindful of my eyes when the subject comes up.

In the church, we were used to having our sisters and brothers in partner congregations include our GDR fate in their thoughts and help carry that weight. And so I suppose I expected the brothers and sisters in the older *Bundesländer* to recognize how much more of the war's aftermath we had had to bear, and therefore to open for us a path to rapid equalization. With great respect I watched as something like a massive deluxe version of the Marshall Plan is helping us make up the distance we had fallen behind. But the distance is not being made up. Instead, we are living through the general collapse of businesses and production sites in the territory of the former GDR. We are watching the monies for the upsurge in the East flowing, through commerce, rapidly back to the West, and the intended upsurge in the East bringing about an upsurge in the West. We are watching as not only assistance from the West, but also a sizeable number of vultures have arrived in our territory. The many pictures of cars left by the side of the road bring to mind images of abandoned, destroyed, burnt-out and rusting military vehicles after World War II. And the imposition of structures from the West German *Länder* strikes me as not a lot different than the imposition back then of structures from the lands of the occupying powers. And not least of all, I was struck by the parallel between the red flags I saw in 1945 with the swastika taken out, and the black, red, and gold flags with the GDR insignia removed. So my estimation of the *Wende* has shifted, so that I can no longer see the *Wende* period as the victory of the new forces in the GDR over the old, failed system. Instead I see it as the East having lost the cold war.

It is my second postwar period. There are winners and losers. Of course, the descent is not the free-fall we experienced in 1945. Of course, for us in the new *Bundesländer* in particular, hopes are substantially more justified than they were for all Germans back then. Of course, I can think of an endless number of cold warriors who poisoned and strangled our life in the GDR era. I know who they are, even as they remain and move among us, now all innocent and peaceable, pretending they had always been that way. But that is also thoroughly familiar from the years after World War II. Back then, too, only the *Führer* was to blame for everything, and mainly the SS was held accountable, rather than those who employed them.

This fundamental change in my estimation of the *Wende* period cost me a great deal of strength. It was forced upon me by many disappointments. And yet it cannot suffocate my basic confidence. For in the end it will – and it must – be true for us all, in East and West, that the lost cold war is not a defeat but a victory for life, as well as a great opportunity for Germany and Europe. I am well aware that, for the citizens of Greifswald and *Vorpommern* during the GDR era, there will be no justice. Nevertheless, in the long term I have no worries about the Hanseatic City of Greifswald and the *Vorpommern* region. They will thrive and flourish.

ABOUT THE AUTHOR

Dr. Reinhard Glöckner received his Dr. theol. in 1962 from the University of Jena. From 1974 to 1990 he was pastor at the *St.-Marien-Kirche* in Greifswald. He was active in the Church's peace movement in the GDR during the 1980s. In 1989 he was involved in organizing peace services and Monday demonstrations in Greifswald. He was part of the Round Table formed to provide guidance to the city administration during the transition. As a founding member of the Council of Counties and Towns in *Vorpommern*, he promoted the interests of the *Vorpommmern* region. He served as mayor of Greifswald from April 1990 to the end of 1992. In 1993, the Ernst Moritz Arndt University in Greifswald named him an honorary senator. The city honored him in 2009 by entering his name into its Golden Book.

ABOUT THE TRANSLATOR

David Ward is Professor of German at Norwich University in Northfield, Vermont, USA.

Made in United States
North Haven, CT
13 November 2023

43975748R00065